DON'T CALL US WE'LL CALL YOU

SOME MEMOIRS OF A MEDIUM

Selena Hart Lubanov

Cover artwork.
Artist Hugh Patterson. Known as 'Shubert'.
Photograph of drawing by Jody Sealwood.

CON-PSY PUBLICATIONS MIDDLESEX

**First Edition
2005**

©Selena Hart Lubanov

This book is copyrighted under the Berne Convention. All rights reserved. No part of this book may be reproduced or utilised in any form or by any means, electronic or mechanical, including photocopying, recording, or by any information storage and retrieval system, without permission in writing from the publisher. Except for the purpose of reviewing or criticism, as permitted under the Copyright Act of 1956.

Published by

CON-PSY PUBLICATIONS

**P.O. BOX 14,
GREENFORD,
MIDDLESEX, UB6 0UF.**

ISBN 1 898680 39 6

CONTENTS

FOREWORD	5
THE POWER OF WORDS	6
CHILDHOOD DREAMS	8
PRANKS BY THE RIVER	10
GRANDMOTHER'S CURE FOR CHILBLAINS	13
SCHOOL BULLIES: NOT A MODERN THING	16
SATURDAY TREATS	21
TIMELESSNESS	23
THE DIFFICULTY OF SEEING THE TRUTH	24
GETTING THE MESSAGE	35
MY FIRST HOME CIRCLE	38
AUTOMATIC WRITINGS AND DRAWINGS BEGIN	41
GLYN'S HELPERS FIND THEIR WAY HOME	45
ANOTHER DRAWING COMES TO LIFE	52
MICHELLE'S KITTEN	55
SPIRIT WILL HAVE THEIR WAY	56
I AM TOLD TO GO HOME	58
NEW HOME NEW CHILD	60
FIRST EXPERIENCE OF SEEING PEOPLE 'EN MASSE'	71
THE EFFECTS OF PREVIOUS LIVES	73
MATCHES AND ROSES	74
FAMILY LINKS THROUGH TELEPATHY?	78
LONDON 1971 HEALING	83
HELPING TO CREATE A YOUNG MILLIONAIRE	86
STREET CONTACT. RUNNING THE HOSTEL	89
FOOTBALL FANS ON THE RAMPAGE	91
EVEN BABIES CAN HEAL	93
HOW SPIRIT MANAGE TO GET THEIR OWN WAY	94
SEEING THINGS AS THEY ARE HAPPENING	100

OPPORTUNITIES THAT SLIP OUT OF TIME -	103
MORE UNBIDDEN MESSAGES - - -	108
EXPERIENCE MUST COME BEFORE KNOWLEDGE	110
WORKING FULL-TIME - - - -	111
A PRAYER GIVEN BY SPIRIT FOR USE IN READINGS	115
"THE MANAGEMENT'S" HELP IN A SEA RESCUE	117
WENDY'S BELL - - - -	121
MEETING THE STARS - - - -	123
TESTIMONIALS - - - -	124
PROOF FOR THE SCEPTICS - - -	125
VOICES OTHER THAN MINE ON THE TAPES -	128
READING FOR A COACH PARTY - -	130
GUIDANCE STRAIGHT FROM THE HORSE'S MOUTH	131
ONE SMALL WORD PROVES SURVIVAL -	132
"DO YOU TELL EVERYONE THE SAME THING?"	133
SHADES OF MURDER - - - -	136
SOME TIME FOR ME? NO - - -	137
HOW IMPORTANT IS OUR NAME? - -	139
OCTOBER SONG - - - -	145
HEALING AND DISAPPOINTMENT IN EASTBOURNE	148
FREEWILL - - - - -	154
WILLING A BOYFRIEND FOR WENDY - -	156
WHY HASN'T IT HAPPENED? - - -	159
WILL I NEVER LEARN? - - -	160
KEITH MOON AND FRIENDS SHOW THE DANGERS -	
OF BAD HABITS	165
YOU MAY FOOL YOURSELVES YOU CAN'T FOOL US!	167
EMILY - - - - - -	169
I DECIDE TO WING IT! - - - -	171
A POEM FOUND IN MY GRANDMOTHER'S BIBLE	175

FOREWORD.

I do not believe there is anything mysterious, miraculous, or, extraordinary about the ability to use the gifts of the Spirit; such as healing, or clairvoyance. To my mind they are simply a continued contact with the fountain of love, the wellspring of all knowledge and power. In essence ALL power is love and light, it is what we as humans do with power that determines whether the end results of thoughts and actions are good or bad.

Some people call this source God, some call on the Buddha, others use the name Allah; different names, but, I maintain, the same power available to all. Whether we are aware of it or not, I am sure that this constant contact is possible for all through what is called Intuition. The ability to listen to our own intuitions is one we all possess to a greater or lesser degree, and sharing my experiences with you is the best way I know to bring this understanding to the surface of the CONSCIOUS mind. I hope it will become easier for you to recognise your own intuitions and follow them.

Intuition is ALWAYS right; if we listen and then act on it we are helped along the path every step of the way. This Intuitiveness, from the subconscious mind, is sometimes called instinct. Instinct is, I believe something which others, or we, train ourselves to obey using the conscious mind. This is what I have tried to explain in the pages that follow, not in an intellectual way because I am in no way qualified to do that, but from my own inadequate attempts to understand a little of what life is all about.

I hope you enjoy reading this book and that it gives you some encouragement to start listening to what I fondly call, 'that little man in my head.' We all may hear or see differently, but as long as we listen, guidance is ours for the taking. Its up to all of us to do the best we can with the life we are given.

THE POWER OF WORDS.

It was a quiet autumn evening and we were gathered together in the back sitting room of the church minister's house. We met there each Thursday evening for prayers and were all members of the Congregational Church. Present on this quiet, calm evening were the minister, Peter Church, his wife Mary, Peter's mother and father, half a dozen other people and myself.

Until THAT Thursday I had always sat quietly, whilst others got to their feet and said their prayers or talked to God in their own way. I had never felt the need to get up or to say anything. I was quite content to sit and bask in the peace created by the prayers flowing from the others in the room. Ah, but now I was on my feet, saying a prayer, an outpouring of love and trust and gratitude, but a prayer I had NEVER heard. I listened in total wonderment.

Where were these words coming from? I did not know. I knew only that I was hearing these gently flowing, powerful words for the first time. That the words were coming from my mouth there was no doubt; yet I had never knowingly heard, or seen, this awesome prayer. The final words of the prayer were said -

"Come, Holy Spirit, come." - and I sat down. As I sat, still in something like a dream, I demanded water. "Water please, somebody get me some water, I need water."

A glass of water was brought to me; and the room was stilled. A calm quiet peace spread through the house and we sat in silence.

Then, as sudden as a summer lightening from a clear blue sky, came the wind, a wind which thundered so loudly it was deafening. It tore through the house; the doors and windows burst open as though a violent storm was raging. Outside all was still; not even the slightest breeze moved the leaves. This continued for some time, the wind creating havoc inside the house, and a calm quiet world outside the windows.

The wind subsided as strangely as it had started for a while the house was still. We sat seemingly transfixed, unable to speak or to move. Then, everyone began to speak at once, excited and yet terrified by what had taken place. When she had recovered sufficiently from the shock, Mrs Church senior rushed over to the piano and began to play a hymn, shouting to everyone as she did so to,

"Sing everyone, sing, come on, sing as loud as you can!"

Later that evening, as we were preparing to leave for our respective homes, Mr Church senior said,

"Well, we ask for the rushing of winds, and when we get it we don't like it!"

Everyone was in a state of consternation, and I was still in that dream-like state that I had been in since the end of my prayer, I had no idea what he was talking about. I heard myself saying,

"If this sort of thing happens here I'm not coming again!" I just wanted to go home to my husband John and my two children.

Until that evening, Mary or one of the other members of the group, had called to take me to the prayer meeting and had driven me home later.

No one came to pick me up the following week, and when I went to Church the next Sunday the minister, and everyone else, seemed so embarrassed, all of them looking the other way rather than catch my eye and have to speak to me. I felt like a leper and decided it would be kinder to everyone if I stayed away.

I found it very difficult to understand the change in these people who I had looked on as my friends. I had been an active member of the church, editing the monthly magazine, taking my turn to provide and arrange the flowers, and helping in any way I could. Being ignored, and feeling so confused about what taken place the previous Thursday evening, I no longer felt a part of this community. Not being welcome at church was a great deprivation for me, and I felt extremely sad.

When I think about it now I realise that this was God's way of showing me that my real work was just beginning, and that this would involve clairvoyance and healing. From now on my life was certainly to be very different.

As a child, I was constantly teased for 'Being different,' for always knowing about things long before they took place, and being aware in a way most people found hard to comprehend. I saw what I called 'peoples lights' and always knew when a person was not telling the truth because their 'lights' changed colour. Every-ones 'lights' were different and I knew what sort of person they were from the colour of their 'lights.'

A change also occurred if someone was ill. If they were very ill, the colour around the area affected would be very dark, almost black, so I always knew without needing to be told. I hated this awareness then and cried myself to sleep on many nights. I wanted to be like everyone else, I wanted to have friends, but I never did. I was always alone, and am still alone.

CHILDHOOD DREAMS.

During my childhood I had a constantly recurring dream, in which I was going to visit a friend of my Mother's, who lived some distance from our house. In my dream I was walking down the road pushing a large doll's pram in which was the biggest, prettiest doll I had ever seen. In reality I owned neither of these things. Oh, I was so happy singing and dancing along the pavement. Suddenly the doll's pram broke loose, running away from me; I chased after it shouting at the top of my voice,

"Come back, come back here this instant; Come back I say."

But it did not come back and I could not catch it. On and on it sped, with me running after it as fast as my little legs could take me. The pram rounded corners, half turning over as it did so, frightening me so much lest it should spill it's precious contents. On and on went the pram at full speed toward a large, gaping hole in the road.

"Stop" I screamed, "Don't go down there, I don't want you to go down there!"

But - down it went. A number of workmen were standing in the road around the edge of that hole, they were laughing and joking with one another. I couldn't stand it and I tugged at their trouser legs, going from one to another screaming at them to rescue my doll's pram and its contents.

"My doll's pram is down your hole, please get it for me, please stop talking and listen to me."

The men continued with their talking and laughing, not taking the slightest notice of me screeching at them. I hit out forcefully at the one nearest me, pummelling his legs as hard as I could. After some minutes of this punishment the man stopped talking to his work-mates, looked down at me and said,

"What's all this racket about? Why don't you go and play with your friends instead of bothering us with your snivelling?"

I continued my blubbering, and pointing to the place where my pram had disappeared down the hole, I said

"My doll's pram has gone down your hole, I want it back, please get it for me."

The workmen tried to find it, but the hole seemed to have become bottomless. I went right on screeching, and was really unhappy. I was feeling very sorry for myself when I became aware of an insistent voice, seeming to come from inside my head, repeating the same sounds over and over again. The voice was telling me to,

"Look over the road dear, turn round, look over the road."

After a while I heard the words clearly enough to understand what

I was supposed to do. I turned, looked, and what I saw filled me with joy. There, stretched before me was a vast expanse of gold shimmering in the sunlight. It was such an amazing sight it took my breath away, so much so that I could no longer scream and shout. I ran across the road, without a care for any traffic there might be; and there to my great delight was a field of golden buttercups, never had I seen a sight so beautiful.

A wooden gate barred my way into the field. I was not tall enough to reach the bolts on the gate, and I could not climb over it. I stood there, wondering how to get into that field. I prayed, no, I pleaded with God to give me a helping hand.

"Please God, help me to get in there somehow. Please, I'll be as good as gold for a whole month if you help me bust into that field."

As I pleaded, I realised I was getting lighter and lighter, so light in fact, that my feet left the ground. Wow, now I was floating, floating light as a feather. I floated up, up and over that tall gate, the gate that a few moments before had barred my way and seemed so impenetrable. Here I was in the field, running among the golden flowers, I gathered armfuls of them to take to my Mother's friend who I had started out to see when I left the house earlier that morning.

No matter how many times I had this dream I never remembered how I got out of the field, but I don't suppose it matters. I always woke up from this dream with the most incredible feeling of joy, which stayed with me.

I was very sure, for the next few hours at least; that no matter what happens all will be well in the end. Nothing lasts forever, good, or bad.

"God's in his heaven, and all's right with the world."

PRANKS BY THE RIVER

The river Chelmer ran through the fields surrounding the farm where I spent my childhood. A lock restricted the flow of the river and she had found a new path off to the right, where she tumbled over steps created by concrete slabs abandoned by the army. These slabs made an artificial waterfall; wonderful for us youngsters. The river joined up with herself a hundred yards or so further on, forming an island in the middle.

At some time during the war the army had built what was called a 'Pill Box' on the island - this was a concrete structure shaped like a bronze three-penny bit, it had slits half way up the walls so the men could see out, and guns could be positioned. This now stood empty and forlorn on the island.

I spent many happy hours sitting under the waterfall having run across the lock gates to get to it. As a child I ran over these gates without a thought of danger, and with great ease. I returned to the spot a few years ago and saw to my horror that the lock gates were less than twelve inches wide and the lock was sixteen feet deep!

Barbara, the girl who lived next door to us, and I, played in and around that waterfall whenever we were allowed some free time.

The journey to the river entailed a fifteen-minute walk from where we lived, past the big pond, then the green pond a little further on. The farm buildings with the pump opposite where we obtained any water that was needed for the house, (no water on tap then!) came next. On down the lane, which led to Tiffin's farm, then across three fields and we were there. Sometimes we were joined by a few boys, we were ten and the boys were mostly teenagers.

Barbara and I always changed into our bathing costumes in the pillbox, leaving our clothes and towels in there, that way they stayed reasonably clean and dry. Most of the boys could swim, but neither Barbara nor I had learned to swim a stroke; we contented ourselves with sitting under, or playing around the waterfall. The two Pratt brothers were quite a bit older, and much more daring, than the rest of us, oh, how we envied them when they did their death defying stunts.

On one memorable hot, sunny day - why is it the days always seemed to be hot and sunny? - I became so impatient with Barbara for taking what seemed like hours to get herself ready to come to the river, that I stormed off in a huff, and went on my own.

When I got to the lock I was not too pleased to see that there were quite a few people there already, including the two Pratt brothers. I crossed the lock, and changed into my costume, leaving my clothes and bag with my towel in it, in the pillbox as usual.

I sat under the waterfall watching the rainbows made by the sun shining through the water. These beautiful rainbows shimmered and danced their way up and down. I had spent an hour or so happily enjoying this spectacle when I saw Barbara coming along the path. She was happily munching away on a carrot which she had pinched from one of Mr Fleming's fields on her way to the river.

The Pratt boys had also seen Barbara with her carrot and they started chasing her to try and steal it.

As Barbara raced across the lock gates to get to me for some support her foot slipped, and still fully clothed, down she went with an almighty splash straight into that sixteen feet of murky grey water!

The boys stood and stared for a few seconds, then fled across the fields as fast as their legs could carry them. Without thinking how we were going to get out, I threw myself into the lock to try and help her. As I have said already neither of us could swim, and to this day I don't know how we got out of that deep grey water. After much kicking and thrashing about we did manage to scramble out unharmed and none the worse for our experience except for being very frightened.

We were both trembling with fear. I instructed Barbara to get out of her wet clothes and use my towel to dry herself. (Barbara's towel had been in her bag which went into the lock with her and to my knowledge was never found.)

Still trembling I dried myself and put my knickers and vest on with just my dress over them. I felt most strange without my petticoat. I had NEVER before ventured outside without it but Barbara's need was greater than my embarrassment. When Barbara had dried herself she covered her nakedness with my petticoat, which was quite voluminous enough to cover her shivering body.

We scurried across the fields, hoping not to meet anyone we knew past Tiffin's farm and on up the lane to her house. What a long journey it seemed the path stretched ahead for what seemed to us in our frightened state to be miles.

Barbara's mother was surprised to see her in my petticoat.

"Where are your own clothes? Not that you don't look snazzy in that outfit, have I missed out on the latest fashions?"

We explained what had happened and luckily for us her Mother was a kind reasonable being and not too cross with her for getting her clothes wet, and losing the 'hold all' and it's contents. This was much more understanding than one thinks when you remember that at the time everything was rationed. Towels shoes hairbrushes and combs were all very difficult, if

11

not impossible, to obtain. She was just glad that Barbara was safe and unharmed. We all had a cup of tea after which we managed to laugh about our experience.

I then put my petticoat on under my dress, and went home. It was more than my life was worth to go home not wearing my petticoat, even though it was only a few yards round the corner. Neither of us told another soul about our adventure. Maybe Barbara has mentioned it to new friends since but I had forgotten all about the adventure until now.

When Barbara and I had talked about it while we were drinking our tea with her Mum, we all decided it was a jolly good job that I had been so cross with her and had stormed off on my own that morning. If I had been with her and still wearing my clothes I would probably have automatically run off with the boys. If I hadn't run, if I'd had time to think things through, I would certainly have been too scared of my Mothers reactions to getting my clothes wet or losing my shoes, which I surely would have done as Barbara had lost hers. I certainly would never have been foolish/brave enough to jump into the river after her.

GRANDMOTHER'S CURE FOR CHILBLAINS.

I suffered with chilblains for most of my childhood. May-be that explains why I was made to wear those thick, black stockings winter and summer?

These painful chilblains sometimes covered my feet and legs from my knees to my toes; they would often become festering, itchy, sores. However this did not prevent me from being sent to school. When my feet were too swollen to fit into my own shoes, the backs of an old pair of someone else's shoes or boots would be cut down. My feet were then shoved into them as far as they would go and off I'd be sent to walk the long road to school. My arms and hands did not escape the ravages of chilblains either. These ugly, painful things covered my hands and arms causing me to cry for days at a time.

My grandmother visited us during the winter months and luckily for me, knew of an old cure for chilblains. Namely, 'Rub all affected parts with freshly fallen snow, DO NOT cover or wrap up in any way, leave to dry naturally.'

I was not at all sure that I liked the sound of that, but said nothing as Grandmother waited patiently, watching from the window. As the first soft snows of the winter fell she called to me,

"Come along child it's time to get rid of those chilblains for ever."

Very reluctantly I removed my shoes and stockings, taking as long as I dared to undo the laces in my shoes, and fumbling with the suspenders that held my stockings up, after all it was very cold out there. Then the rest of my clothing was removed by my Grandmother, leaving me as naked as the day I was born.

I was playfully half dragged, half carried out to the garden, and the cold new snow was rubbed well in to every part of me, not a crack or crevice was left untreated by my Grandmother.

It was not until she was convinced that every inch of my exposed body had been rubbed with the freezing snow that I was allowed back indoors. I then had to wait until my skin had well and truly dried itself, before being allowed to put my clothes back on.

A very painful but extremely effective treatment I have never had a chilblain since. Touch wood.

Grandmother stayed with us for a few weeks after this treatment. During her stay she and I were walking home from a journey to Chelmsford market and she needed to spend a penny. She decided she would find a quiet spot in the garden of the now empty thatched cottage that had once belonged to the Holdens.

The Holdens were a brother and sister in their eighties whose family had lived in that thatched cottage for hundreds of years. However, the council had insisted that the cottage was uninhabitable, and they must leave the only home they'd ever known, and leave NOW. The cottage was condemned and closed up, a large iron S shape was hammered into the walls to show it could no longer be lived in. Though many people had protested that the council was being inhumane in making these elderly people leave the home they loved and cherished for over ninety years, they were adamant. The Holdens were moved to a newly built council house at the other end of the lane, four miles away.

Before they had been so cruelly uprooted I often used to visit them in their thatched cottage. The rooms were small with heavy oak-beams. A fire burned continuously in the open grate of the comfortable living room, but the place to head for when it was cold outside was the kitchen. The black-leaded kitchen range glowed with the heat of a roaring fire which, not only heated the room; it also heated the ovens and the top of the stove. On this there was always a large iron pot. Simmering in it would be a delicious soup, made from whatever was edible and available at the time. Vegetables and herbs from the garden, bones and anything else, which added bulk and flavour where used in the making of this soup. As some of the soup was consumed other ingredients and more liquid would be added, the pot was never empty. Wonderful smells escaped from this simmering pan through a hole in the lid. Many years ago there had been a knob here, but this had broken off with constant use. Now that tantalising aroma, carried in the steam escaping through that convenient hole, wafted through the door of the kitchen, and made one feel exceedingly hungry. Whenever I called in, I was offered a good-sized bowl of this wholesome, nutritious soup.

Butterflies and moths collected over the centuries, were pinned to the walls and ceilings of the thatched cottage, or preserved in specimen trays. When the Holdens were forcibly moved, it was to prove impossible to remove any of these beautiful creatures from the walls or beams, without them breaking up, so the old couple travelled with just the few treasures which were in the specimen trays. They went to the cold, modern eyesore of a council house with all mod cons, none of which they wanted or knew how to use. As you can imagine they were both terribly miserable, and neither of them wanted to go on living. They longed for the comfort of their small warm, thatched cottage they had known all their lives. Mr Holden died of a broken heart a few weeks after being moved. Miss Holden decided that she would not stay on this earth without him. A fortnight after he had died she put on her Sunday best clothes, left the cold impersonal council house - and walked along the lane as far as she could in the direction of her beloved thatched cottage. Not being able to walk any further she sat under a hedge and waited to die. She was found some weeks later by Mr Bird the road sweeper.

The cottage withstood the might of the Germans bombs, all the ravages of nature, (human and animal) for many years until it was finally bulldozed to make way for a new road. Mr and Miss Holden could, and should, have been left to spend the last few years of their lives in the peace and comfort of their own beloved thatched cottage.

After they had died I was sure I often 'saw' them in the garden, walking and talking with each other, as I passed by on my way to and from school. I often sat in that cottage garden and talked with them, telling them everything that was happening to me, all my joys and my woes, sure that they heard and answered me. I always asked their permission, before eating any of the fruit or vegetables, which grew abundantly for years.

Now to get back to the day on which I started this story of the Holdens, and my grandmother's need to spend a penny rather badly. Grandmother told me to keep a lookout as she secreted herself behind one of the thick hedges in the Holdens garden, hiding herself from anyone who might be passing by in the lane. Up came her skirts, and her three petticoats with lace round the hems, and undone was the ribbon, which held up her drawers! No elastic to be had in those days of scarcities, most of the time tape was used, but these were her Sunday best drawers.

I knew Mr Holdens Spirit would be very embarrassed to see my Grandmother hitching up her clothes and pulling down her drawers! Oh dear, what could I do now? It was all very embarrassing for me! I had never imagined that my Grandmother had to do things like that - like going to the loo I mean. I thought only ordinary people like me did that. Grandmother was like the Queen to me, and I was pretty sure that SHE didn't do things as common place as that!

SCHOOL BULLIES: NOT A MODERN THING

I attended a small Church school for a couple of years, but received very little formal education as there were few teachers, and the school coped with all the local pupils aged from four to fourteen. The Head Mistress, Miss Cutts, taught me to use her sewing machine. I ran errands for her and did a number of other things, none of which helped me intellectually then or later in life.

I had quite a good singing voice and was often made to stand at the front of the whole school and sing songs like, 'All through the night.' I didn't see this as a drawback at the time, because sewing and singing got me out of having to do P T and playing boisterous games which I hated.

My classmates called me 'teachers pet,' I certainly didn't want to be. I wanted to be like the others but I was not like them. I disliked noise even then never wanting to run about or shout preferring to be still and watch others. I have always enjoyed watching other people do things rather than participate in activities, especially those which meant I would have to make a noise. Neither could I bear to tear the wrapping paper off anything, even sweets. I always undid things very carefully, and saved the paper, still do, just in case it's needed for something later on.

I wore thick, black stockings, winter and summer. They were very uncomfortable in summer as you can imagine, but it didn't occur to me to take them off, I had been told to wear them, so wear them I did. I was teased unmercifully by the other girls, who either wore white socks, or went barelegged in the summer.

When my maternal Grandmother was staying with us she became concerned when she heard me in tears night after night, and demanded to know the reason for my distress. I confessed to her that it was because I was being teased continuously over having to wear those thick black stockings in the hot weather, and could she PLEASE do something about it! What she did do only made things worse. She wrote a letter to Miss Cutts, telling her of my distress! What I had wanted her to do was to ask my Mother not to make me wear those dreadful stockings! During assembly the following morning my name was called, and I was ordered by Miss Cutts to,

"Come up here girl and stand next to me."

Up to the front of the hall I went, 'all unsuspecting', while teachers and children giggled, and whispered amongst themselves. The letter was taken from its envelope, and read out to the whole school. I squirmed, but to no avail.

"Point out those children who have made your life so unhappy; come along girl, say who they are. - Or don't you have the courage to do even that?"

Obviously she also considered that I was a wimp, having to get my grandmother to write a letter, instead of standing up for myself! I could not give the names, not for any moralistic reasons, simply because I was scared stiff, and worried about being disliked more than I was already. Of course it didn't help at all, they then called me a coward as well as a wimp. No one would speak to me unless they had too!

There were some evacuees from London attending our school since the authorities had decided that as many children as possible should be moved to the comparative safety of the country. Georgina was one of these young people; just a couple of years older than I, she had beautiful long golden hair, and as she bounced along it shone and glistened like burnished gold in the sun. If the truth be known it was probably because who-ever was looking after her made sure her hair was washed and rinsed thoroughly every day!

She also had a gleaming new bicycle. Up until then, the only ones to own bicycles were a few of the older boys. They often passed me on my way to school clinging to the backs of lorries or buses. 'Cadging a lift' is what they called this highly dangerous practice. I must admit they got to school much more quickly that way and with very little effort from them!

I NEVER saw Georgina RIDE her bicycle, she would either wheel it in that stately manner of hers, or allow one of the others, who was favoured by her that day, wheel it for her. Georgina showed her favour by being especially nice to that person. The rest of us who were 'out' of favour tagged along behind. Oh, how I longed to be one of her 'favoured' ones. I followed her everywhere like a large ungainly puppy, wearing ill-fitting clothes, and with untidy, unkempt hair hanging around my shoulders, how revolting I must have seemed to her. Luckily I was unaware of how I looked, so it did not concern me.

Each day on our way home from school, we walked in the same direction until we reached the lane, which led to the farm where I lived. I turned off down the lane, and Georgina continued along the main road until she reached her 'billet.' On the day of 'the letter' when I had refused to name the ones who had made my life hell, I was, as always, trotting along behind Georgina with the other children who travelled home along the same road. There we all were, trailing in her glory. When she became aware that I was there behind her with the rest of the gang she stopped in her tracks, turned sharply on her heels and said to me,

"Don't walk behind me, I don't want you anywhere near me. I don't like you; in fact, I dislike you intensely. Not only are you a telltale, you're a coward as well, you make me sick. Go to the other side of the road and walk by yourself, maybe that will help you to learn to stand up for yourself!"

She refused to continue her journey until I had dutifully crossed to the opposite side of the busy main road, to the jeers and shouts of derision from the ones who were allowed to continue to walk with her. When I was far enough away from her Georgina tossed her beautiful golden hair and continued on her stately way with the others who, like me, clamoured for her attention walking proudly behind their leader. I decided that I really MUST learn to stand up for myself.

The school we all attended was 'mixed' and for pupils between the ages of four and fourteen. There were four classrooms and a fair sized hall, which could be divided up when necessary, by closing the central sliding doors. This hall also became the gymnasium for PT lessons. A large field was our playground. In this field were plenty of large trees to play in, and around. The ugly air-raid shelters and outside loos were hidden from sight by these trees, so even they couldn't spoil the pleasure of sitting in that place for me. We had none of the swings, sea-saws, swimming pools, or other accruements that people seem to think are necessary for children these days. It was an ideal setting in which to spend one's childhood. The school was two or three miles from my house, and it seemed a very long walk to me as a child. I sang at the top of my voice to keep myself company, I also thought,

'If I stop singing someone will know I'm being attacked and come and rescue me.'

Quite often during the winter it was dark by the time we were let out of school at the end of the afternoon, and I was terrified when walking down the lane alone. The lane to the farm was quite narrow with ditches and high hedges on both sides. There were no signposts or road signs of any sort anywhere, this was so 'strangers' wouldn't know where they were. The signs had all been removed 'for the duration of the war' never to be replaced. We were all told that we must never talk to strangers, our instructions were,

"If anyone asks the way to anywhere you must not say, "I don't know" - that would be telling a lie. You may say, "I'm sorry, but I can't say." You must be careful these people may be German spies!"

So here we were, in the heart of the country, being told there might be German spies round the corner! No wonder I was terrified.

An AA man known to all of us, and who was always very kind to me, stood outside his bright yellow kiosk on the corner of the Arterial road most days. This road met the main road, along which we walked to and from school every day, we were always pleased to see him and I for one, was very disappointed when he wasn't there. In his yellow kiosk there was a telephone so that he could call for assistance if a motorist needed help. Very few people had telephones and when he used it we all wanted to listen in. He wore a very smart yellow uniform, and saluted every car bearing an AA Badge. If all was well with the driver and his car, the driver returned the AA mans salute. I used to muse on how wonderful it would be when I grew up to own a car with an AA badge, (I thought it must, at the very least, mean that person was very important) and have someone like this man salute me. If there was not much traffic and he had nothing else to do, he would lift me up onto the seat of his bicycle. Then he'd wheel me some of the way to school, telling me funny stories, or poems, that he had made up while he was waiting for a car to come along. I'm sure I never knew this man's name, I still think of him a lot and remember his kindness to me in the otherwise harsh and unfriendly world of which I was a part, and in which I spent my childhood.

Over the years people who have clairvoyant powers, have told me of seeing a man in a yellow uniform. This, 'the 'YELLOW' uniform' quite often puzzles them, as they don't associate yellow with uniforms.

These clairvoyants say that the man comes to salute me. I like to think it's my friend from the AA. I hope it is, because that would mean he survives somewhere, and also remembers me, a scruffy, unhappy little schoolgirl.

When I was not at school, I spent as much time as I could wandering about the fields, sometimes helping with the haymaking.

I took flasks of tea and picnic baskets full of sandwiches to the men during haymaking, if it was very hot, I took a large jug of sparkling homemade lemonade instead of the hot tea. That's if anyone had enough sugar to make it. The men would never stop working until the whole field was cut in case the weather changed and the hay was ruined. The tractor used for cutting the hay circled the field, starting at the edge of the field and getting closer to the centre with each circuit. When it had almost reached the centre, the farm hands spread themselves out round the edge of the circle and began to beat the ground with the large sticks they had brought with them for the purpose of killing the rabbits. Meat was rationed, and quite often impossible to get, and a rabbit or two made a jolly good nutritious stew.

The rabbits had all run to the centre of the field to get away from the machine's blades. With each circuit they bunched closer together sheltering in what long grass was left. Now, with the giant noisy, thing just a few yards away from them, there was nothing else for it but to break cover and run, run as fast as they could. They ran in their terrified state, trying to dodge out of the way of the men with their sticks. These sticks all had a fat, heavy head on the end of them, like a club. If the rabbits were unlucky enough to get caught they were clubbed to death with swift hard blows to the head, or whichever part the men could hit. I tried to avoid going to the field when the tractor was nearing the middle; because I knew that I would be given a stick and made to stand guard on the edge of the circle, to help the others prevent the rabbits escaping. It was a them or me situation really. If I let the rabbits go I was for it, and I would get the stick. If I stopped them they would surely end up in the stew-pot, and I would save myself a beating. So you can see why I didn't like to be around the field near the end of haymaking! It was a time of war and we were constantly being urged to save everything we didn't need for ourselves, including bones from any meat we had, and the peelings from the fruit and vegetables. 'Waste not, want not, put it in the pig-pot' - was seen on posters everywhere. Men came with lorries to empty the 'pig-pots' every few days. What a smell!

SATURDAY TREATS.

The W.V.S. paid a shilling for a bag of hips and haws, both of which could be collected from the hedgerows with a little bit of effort. They also paid for conkers. I can understand now why they wanted hips and haws, these were used to make a very valuable syrup for children, but conkers? Why did they want conkers? I have never found anyone who could tell me how conkers helped with the war effort.

Saturday morning became a wondrous time for me if I had been able to collect enough hips and haws to fill a fairly large bag. I started out very early for the walk into Chelmsford to deliver the bag of hips and haws to the W.V.S shop on the High Street. If the bag was full enough and big enough they gave me a silver shilling. I then hurried on to the Co-op bakery situated behind the main railway station at the other end of town. Every Saturday morning, (it may have happened every morning but I only knew about Saturdays) the sales staff opened a large hatch at the side of the building and sold what were called stale cakes. These were the cakes that had been left unsold in the shops the day before, and had been returned to the bakery. If I didn't get there early enough I had a very long wait, and I was always scared they would run out of cakes before I reached the hatch. Sometimes the queue stretched as far as the Railway station buildings a good hundred yards up the road. I was not supposed to be there at all, and certainly couldn't wait too long. If my Mother had found out I'd been to the city, I would most certainly have been in a lot of trouble. The stick would have been brought out from its place by the side of the fireplace and I, oh no you don't want to hear about that. As you can imagine I tried to be among the first to arrive. The procedure was thus, I handed over my precious shilling, in return they gave me a silver sixpence change, and a very large bag bursting with cakes. Every sort of cake you can imagine was there on those shelves, and the sooner I got to the front of the queue the better the selection would be. Of course I was not allowed to choose which ones I wanted the person who was serving me did that, but I am sure they always tried to give me the best cakes! I enjoyed what ever I was given, and I devoured every one of them on my journey home. The next port of call after I had been given the cakes, was the bus station, just across the road from the railway station. There I boarded a bus, using some of the remaining six pence to pay my fare. How very important I felt sitting on the top deck of an Eastern National bus and paying my own fare. I alighted from the bus one stop before reaching Pump Lane, which was where I would get off if I was going straight home, and made my way to Miss Clark's emporium. Miss Clark had most of the children's sweet coupons and had been given complete control of when or how many, sweets we could have. I think as children we were all allowed four ounces a week officially, but I'm pretty certain Miss Clark gave most of us a few extra ounces occasionally. It was here in this Aladdin's cave that I spent the last of my hard-earned shilling. Sweets were always served in what was called a 'poke.' A poke was a square of paper, which was rolled round the hand in a certain way, and ended up looking like an upside-down pyramid. The pointed end was then twisted and turned up so the sweets could not fall out of the bottom. Bags were a very rare commodity and seldom seen except in places like the bakers.

Miss Clark's family had been here in this shop, and had lived behind and above it for as long as anyone could remember. Miss Clark and her two brothers continued the tradition. They were all single and now getting toward old age, but the brothers still chopped and sawed the wood, which was stacked up at the back of the shop. Inside the shop there were always smells of kindling wood, paraffin, soap powders, and coal all mixed up with the biscuits, fruit, dairy produce, sugar, oh, and a hundred other things people needed to survive. The Messrs Clark sold it all; it was the only general store for miles. There was a tobacconists, the 'Wilkinsons,' just round the corner but no other 'general' store.

TIMELESSNESS

My childhood aloneness was necessary as it allowed me to be aware of the beauty of the world about me. If I had been constantly involved in a state of activity with others, it may have developed my personality, but I feel that it would have been at the expense of my psyche. The wanderings through the fields alone gathering hips and haws; sitting under the waterfall watching the sun through the water; resting quietly in the churchyard, all were contacts with truth through nature, not activity of the personality. If I had been surrounded by friends, or if I'd had parents who pushed me towards intellectual development, I may not have seen the wonder of leaves unfolding as I sat watching, activity would have diverted my attention.

Our personality grows throughout our life, formed as the years pass by. But, I believe, that our psyche is mature at conception, and brings with it memories of past lives. Our psyche works in a timeless way, whereas our personality is determined by the movement of time. We make goals for ourselves, or keep returning to past disappointments, when we insist on going over our past mistakes with our thoughts and words, and we perpetuate that way of being. We find the same sort of things happening over and over again, in other words we keep ourselves in that cycle. We think it would be difficult to change our thought pattern, the mind gets used to working in a particular way and we insist that it would be hard to change that pattern, but it's the thinking about changing that's the difficult part the doing is easy! In psychic matters we are in a timeless state, apart from time and distance. When someone we love is sick, or involved in trouble of some kind, we know, the instant it happens. The message comes winging to us cutting through the barriers of time and space, no matter how far they are from us. At these times we are operating 'out of time.' Our conscious mind plays no part in any of this.

We suffer from disease when we insist on living in a time bound state, constantly surrounded by noise and activity. If we would just take some time out to be quiet we'd find we feel so much better. 'Be still and know that I am' still holds true.'

THE DIFFICULTY OF SEEING THE TRUTH.

I firmly believe 'THE' truth can not be A truth. The truth is absolute. I can hear you saying, "That's not right, everyone sees things differently, truth is not the same for all of us." I agree, but I still say 'THE' truth is absolute. Of course we all have our own interpretations of things, we all see things differently, and thank the Lord for that, but it's just our personal interpretation of what we see. Things are coloured by the way we have been taught to observe our surroundings. So often after an incident the Police are given so many differing accounts of the event, simply because everyone has vividly remembered some aspect of that event, very seldom does any one see the whole incident. It does not alter the facts, the truth, of the event. The facts are the facts. The truth is the truth. For example, the police are informed that a man has been beaten up; one witness will say, "His attacker was wearing a blue sweater and grey jeans, and just struck out for no reason." Another will say, "No, the man was acting in self defence, the 'victim' hit out first." Both are pretty sure of their facts, and yet they can't both be right in their interpretations. The truth is, A man has been injured in a fight or a brawl of some kind, both of the witnesses saw the same incident but from a different standpoint, each one sure of what they thought they saw, and for them of course it was the truth.

When wandering the fields as a child, I was not to know how important my experiences would prove to be later. It was absolutely necessary for me to retain my contact with those aspects of truth through nature, to enable me to help people in psychic ways as a channel for healing and clairvoyance. I am sure I don't do as much as I could for 'The Management', as I like to call those who work through me. I feel I let them down quite often, but I try and take heart from those who say that they were helped beyond measure, by a word, or a sentence, that I have not even been aware of saying. And, many people say, they can pinpoint a turning point in their lives to just that time. I have reached the conclusion that we help others much more when we are not trying to help, than we do when we try and work things out using our conscious mind. When we try so hard, we are, more often than not, simply arguing with ourselves. 'Shutting the top of our head' and so failing to see, or to hear, the answers that really are sitting there waiting for us thereby creating more difficulties. We are using the personality when we do that, and standing in our own light.

I had got myself into just that sort of state, 'standing in my own light' a few years ago, and decided to visit an astrologer Howard Sasporter, who had been recommended to me. He spent some time explaining the positions of the planets in the heavens at the time of my birth, none of which I made any sense to me. He took great care to try and help me understand what he was saying by drawing maps and graphs; after some time he asked, "What happened to you when you were eleven or twelve? Something drastic was going on which had the effect of holding you back." You can read what that was on the following pages. I told him what had happened.

His reply was, "Surely you understand that your paralysis was caused by your mind saying to your body, 'Hey, hang on, just a minute, I haven't had my childhood yet, I don't want to go into puberty. Please let me have some fun first, I don't want to grow up so fast!"

These words were a great revelation to me, they explained so many hitherto puzzling aspects of my psyche. They helped me to understand, allowing me to see why, to this day, I can not pass a children's playground without longing to go on the swings. If I am very lucky there is no attendant on duty, and I can soar as high as the swing will allow, rejoicing in the sense of freedom and fun it gives me.

Around the time of my coming up to my eleventh birthday, the education committee decided that all children of eleven years and over must leave the local Church schools and attend Moulsham School, six miles away on the other side of Chelmsford. The other children's parents called for a meeting to decide how we were supposed to get there and back home again at the end of the day's work. After all there was a war on and it was a long journey for young people to make on their own. The consensus of opinion was that all children would be excluded from any school until the authorities provided a bus to get us all there, and back to our homes after school. The negotiations between the Bus Company and the local authorities dragged on for months. Where would the petrol for the buses come from? Who would pay for these buses? Whose staff wanted to be responsible for dozens of screaming kids? And so on, and so on.

I was nearing my twelfth birthday by the time every one was satisfied and a bus service was provided for us. It was most exciting, travelling all that way on a bus without a conductor asking for; 'Fare's please.' On arriving at this vast complex of modern buildings, confusion reigned, I was taken one way and the others from Springfield School went in a different direction. I found later that I was in a class for the older children, 3b. The others went to 1a or 1b, being 'teachers pet' had done me no good yet again! In the eyes if the others I was being given preferential treatment. I was distraught after all I had done nothing to warrant being singled out. Maybe being taller than most of the others made me seem older! I had only been attending this school for a few weeks, and trying very hard to study and learn as much as I could, when large painful abbesses came up on my heels which made it impossible for me to walk.

Within a week my mouth was closed tight, eclampsia I believe they called it, by abbesses in the gums. As I could not walk, my heels being so inflamed, the family physician Doctor Alford, was called out to the farm.

He lanced the abscesses on the heels, and then advised my Mother to hire a car and take me to a dentist in the city to have the ones in my mouth treated. The dentist broke one of my front teeth trying to get at the abscess but I was in so much pain he found it impossible to do any thing. Dr Alford came to the farm again the next day and gave me an injection to clear the poisons from my body. Then, from his pocket he produced two fresh hen's eggs, the only eggs available to us during the war were dried, and came from a packet, so it was quite a pleasurable shock to see these brown eggs nestling in his hand. He explained that he kept hens in his back garden and the eggs from these hens were collected for the Ministry of Food. Today he had decided that my need was greater than the Ministries. He asked my mother for a bowl, cracked the eggs on the side of it, emptied the contents into the bowl, and carefully put the now empty eggshells into his pocket! Seeing the shocked look on my face, (I would have been in trouble if I'd put eggshells in my pockets;) and smiling at my confusion, he explained,

"The eggshells will be crushed and added to the hen's food in the morning, they need a bit of grit you know."

It seemed very strange to me that the hens may be eating their own eggshells tomorrow! While he was explaining this to me, he was busy whisking the eggs in the bowl to a smooth mixture. He then sat opposite me and told me to open my mouth as far as I could. "Come along now my girl, open wide."

By this time, however, I had indeed developed eclampsia. Yes, that's what it was, and I could not move my jaws to open my mouth. He gently tipped my head back, and spooned the egg mixture between my closed teeth, until the last drop had slipped down my throat. Dr Alford came to the house and repeated this process every day for the next five days; he also made sure that I was given enough fluids. My Mother told me that he gave me the eggs personally to make sure that it was indeed me who had the eggs, and not my stepfather. I felt that my mother had quite enough to do without having to look after me as well. Washing needed to be done every day; the water for this was fetched from the pump down the lane, and heated up in the copper, which stood in the corner of the kitchen. Meals had to be prepared for the family with whatever food was available, and cooked on the kitchen range, and the hundred and one other things a wife and mother has to do daily. So I stayed in my room as much as possible, and made not a sound if I could help it. I didn't feel sorry for myself; indeed, I much preferred to be in my room, away from the heat of the copper in the kitchen, and out of my stepfather's reach.

Most of the food my mother managed to obtain using the ration books was eaten by my stepfather. He was working and needed it more than we did; no one questioned this. In those days children did not question what was said by grown ups - 'They must know best, of course.'

On Sunday mornings I was occasionally allowed to have some butter on my bread, wonderful tasty butter. At all other times it was margarine if I was lucky. But on these, what were to me, momentous occasions, I ate this bread and butter with another rare treat, an apple from the orchard. During the months of September and October if I got up early enough, around four-thirty, I went out into the fields and cut myself some mushrooms. Large, white field mushrooms, delicious. I then had to hurry back to the house, cook and eat them before my stepfather came back from early morning milking, otherwise he would most certainly have laid claim to them!

But to return to my abscess's, when they had healed it was decided that I could return to school the next week, I was overjoyed, I couldn't bear being shut up in the house, any thing was better than that, even School. My joy was short lived, for, over the next few hours my skin turned a very nasty shade of yellow and I was promptly put back to bed. Yellow jaundice was diagnosed and I became extremely ill. I have wondered since, whether having nothing but eggs for so long had anything to do with it? When the jaundice had cleared and it was time for me to start getting up for a while, it became increasingly clear that my legs would not do what I wanted them to, and I soon could not move them at all.

I was taken to hospital in Chelmsford, where it was decided that I had Infantile paralysis, now called Polio. The specialist, Mr Camp thought that being undernourished might have had something to do with my contracting this illness. As I was almost twelve years old now, it was the women's ward for me. I was carried up to the ward at the front of the hospital on the top floor, overlooking the main London road. The recreation grounds stretched for a mile or so behind the hospital, and in these grounds there was an 'Ack-Ack' station. Further over was the main railway station; the Germans were always trying to bomb one or other, or both, and sometimes hit the hospital instead. Many patients came and went during my long stay in that hospital women's ward. Some left to go home, walking out happily with their families or friends. Whilst others, far too many for my liking, were taken out in that box-like thing which the porters brought into the ward on a stretcher. This was put to use whenever a patient had died. The nurses always tried very hard to hide this from us, sometimes even waiting until night-time to take the body out, hoping that we would be asleep and not notice what was happening. But I always knew, I knew days before the nurses were aware of this person's imminent death, because I saw their 'lights' going out.

A Mrs Turner was in the bed next to me when I first went into hospital; she was very friendly helping me to settle in, and to understand the routine. A few weeks later she was told that she could go home the next day, both she and I were overjoyed at first thinking it was because she was now recovered. Later that day I watched her lights getting dimmer and I knew that she had cancer, and she would certainly die very soon. Her family was being allowed to take her home for the last few days of her life. I did not want to let her see that I was unhappy, and tried very hard not to cry - but I could not stop the tears from flowing. I think I convinced her that I was crying because I would miss her cheerful company, and did not want her to leave me.

Julie worked in the Pathological Laboratories at the other end of the hospital. One of her duties was to visit the wards and take samples of blood for analysis, on a visit to one of the wards she caught a virus, was brought into our ward amid great excitement, and put into a small curtained area at the beginning of the main ward. As she recovered the curtains were drawn back, and from my bed I could see her sitting at her bed-table, drawing and painting. Nurse Turner brought some of Julie's drawings for me to look at; they were mainly of flowers and landscapes, and I thought they were exquisite.

All the staff at the hospital had been working very long hours without sufficient rest or nourishment, and quite a number of them had become ill. The Matron sent a junior round to all the wards bringing a notice that read,

"Except in an emergency, no member of staff will be on duty for longer than eight hours, and all staff must make sure that they are properly nourished."

But as there was 'a state of emergency most of the time, the directive did not have much effect! Consequently the nurses went right on 'catching' one thing after another.

One morning after an exceptionally bad night of air raids, someone was brought into the ward and put into the bed next to mine. The curtains around her bed remained firmly closed, which puzzled me, but not one person would tell me why. As the weeks went by she had .no visitors, and I felt really sorry for her. I kept up a constant stream of chatter, telling her everything that was happening in the ward - who was coming - who was going, what they did and said - and, what I thought about it all! There was never any response from behind the curtains, but I kept right on chattering away to this person that I didn't know, and had not seen. No one would tell me anything about her, or why she was in hospital, so I tried to find out. The curtains remained closed and I was bursting with curiosity. But still all lips stayed firmly sealed. This frustrating situation continued for several more weeks, until, a week before my thirteenth birthday there was a tremendous amount of activity behind those seemingly impenetrable curtains surrounding her bed.

After what seemed to me like an eternity, I heard her curtains being pulled back - first on the side away from my bed, oh, why don't they do this side first, and then with a swish, rattle, swish, the one on my side was slowly pulled back.

I waited, with barely suppressed excitement to see who would come out from behind the curtains. What I did see filled me with awe. Out came two Nuns in flowing black habits, one Nun leading the other, holding very carefully on to the others arm - the one being led asked to be brought to my bedside. She asked her companion to put her hand in mine, and then, in a barely audible voice, she said to me. "I hear it's your birthday next week - what would you like? I'd really like to give you something for saving my life."

"Oh, but, but, I haven't done anything." I stammered.

"Yes you have, my child. You saved my life. You kept me interested in what was going on out here in the ward with your chatter, and in spite of my ardent wish to die, I had to stay alive to hear what happened next! Tell me, what would you like most in all the world for this important birthday of yours?"

"Oh! Well then, I'd like an autograph book please, if that's all right."

"Of course that's all right! You shall have one. My friends are taking me to London now, and I will make sure one is sent to you from there."

As the two Nuns were leaving, I suddenly realised what I had been doing.

"I have been talking to a Nun! Oh my goodness, ordinary people just don't talk to Nuns - Nuns are a part of God. I'm sure God will strike me dead. What have I done? Ah, but then she did say I'd saved her life, so - maybe he'll see fit to forgive me."

One of the nurse's came and comforted me after the two nuns had left, and said that she could now tell me the nuns story. She told me, "The convent where our nun had been in service received a direct hit by a very powerful new bomb, one of the first 'Doodle-bugs' I think, and she was one of the few survivors. Her arms and legs had been badly mutilated, and her eyes severely damaged. Her friend is taking her to an eye specialist in London to try and save her sight." There was nothing more that could be done for her in our hospital. My chattering had been an important part of her stay with us, giving her the will to live when all she wanted was to die and join her friends who had died in that air raid. Who else would have been so unaware of the usual social rules? - Rules that tell us, 'Do not speak to strangers,' 'Speak only when we are spoken too,' and yes, 'To keep quiet if we are given no encouragement.' I was so socially unaware that I just continued to chatter. But, was I so unaware? Or, aware unknowingly, even then?

Margaret McClain was in the A T S and was brought into hospital with a painful, septic rash which covered her hands and arms. I'm sure that can't be all that was wrong with her, but that is all I was told. She quite often sat by my bed telling me about her family seat in Scotland, and how she longed to be there. Grapevines planted by her ancestors ran over the hills leading from her house to the loch. She helped me to see the beauty of Fife with her flowing graphic descriptions. I was invited to visit her and her family when the war was over. No, I never did I lost the address.

Margaret also left the ward that week, fully recovered, to rejoin her unit, and went promising to send me some sticks of rock for my birthday. The war continued and sweets were still rationed so I had not seen a stick of rock for years. I certainly could not remember when I had last tasted peppermint rock. So instead of being sad that Margaret was leaving me, I looked forward to receiving the peppermint rock. On the morning of my birthday two parcels arrived both of them oblong and flat. But one parcel was slightly thicker than the other. I decided to open the thinnest one first and inside was a beautiful, red leather covered autograph book from the Nun. Oh what joy, she has remembered me.

My fingers lingered lovingly over this book and I thought how wonderful it was to have something of my own; something new, which no other person had used. I had never before owned anything new.

I did not want to let go of this beautiful object but I did so long to open the other parcel, which was sitting on the top of the bedside cupboard. I waited. For as long as I could hold out I waited, fantasising about the delicious peppermint rock hiding under all that brown paper and string! - How my mouth watered! I could stand the temptation no longer I laid the book down very carefully and tore away at the other parcel; first the string, why oh why did there have to be so many yards of it? Then at the brown paper layers of it and there, there was the tin proclaiming 'Edinburgh Rock.' I had waited so long for this moment looking forward to tasting the pink, brittle peppermint rock. I was so sure it would be pink on the outside and white inside, with letters running through the middle. I wondered what the letters would say. Will they say Edinburgh? - Fife? - Scotland?

I had seen that rock so often in my mind during the week leading up to my birthday, and now all I had to do was open the tin nestling in my hands. I prised the tin open, could not contain my excitement a moment longer, not even long enough to examine the rock, I took a large piece and put it in my mouth. Strange flavours run round my teeth and gums. What was this? The rock was sweet and soft, not peppermint rock at all, but something completely different. What I had in my mouth was Scottish Rock! Oh, how disappointed I was. I cried for hours, I had so looked forward to peppermint rock. I distressed myself so much that I brought on a soaring temperature, the nurses were all very worried and tried everything they could think of to pacify me. But I continued crying and making myself ill. Then someone had the bright idea of taking my autograph book round the ward.

A 'wall of friendship' where everyone wrote their name on one of the bricks, was started, and Nurse Turner chose a blue page on which to write.

"Be good sweet maid, and let who will be clever. Do noble things, not dream them all the day."

She could not get the rest of the verse on the page, but said that that was quite enough for me to be getting on with for today!

Another patient wrote, "True friends are like diamonds, precious and rare; false friends are like autumn leaves, found everywhere."

Mrs Curtis wrote on the last page, "By hook or by crook I'll be last in this book!"

Julie painted some roses on one page and the most beautiful pink and red carnations on another. By this time Julie had recovered sufficiently to work part-time in the laboratories again, but still had to return to the ward to sleep when she had finished her duties. She was still not fit enough to be discharged, but, the hospital was very short staffed and everyone, including Julie, did all they could to make sure patients were given everything they needed to hasten their recovery and discharge. Julie worked for a few days, but still being in such a weak state after her illness; she caught another virus, so it was back to bed in the ward full-time for her!

I was happy in one way that she was back, because I had missed her cheerful face, but very sad that she was ill again.

Julie died two days later.

I was devastated by her death. I had seen a great many people die during my long stay in the hospital, but Julie, my sweet, pretty, kind, young Julie. She was in her early twenties, and always doing everything she could to help both nurses and patients. Never a scowl or a long face. WHY? Oh why, did my Julie have to die? As far as I knew, she had never harmed anyone.

Nurse Turner sat with me, night and day, over the next week, giving me support and comfort. She tried explaining why we die, and told me that we will all die when its our time to die, no matter how good or perfect we strive to be, or how much of our time we spend in the service of our fellow travellers on the way.

I decided then and there, that there was obviously no point in doing what I was told, being good, or helping anyone, if that was all there was to it. I might just as well lie and cheat my way through life, and be really horrible. If I could not die now and be with Julie that was exactly what I would do. All I wanted to do was to die, and die NOW.

I was told by Nurse Turner.

"That's a wicked thing to want, you will die when it's your time to die, not when you want to! It's a sin to wish your life away!"

I did not care and I still insisted that I was going to die and the sooner the better! It was not until I saw how much my behaviour was upsetting everyone in the ward, and how unbearably distressed Nurse Turner was becoming that I accepted what she was telling me. I promised that I would go on living, and try to be good, until it was my time to die.

I learned later that Nurse Turner had given up all her off-duty time to be there during that time of horror for me. She was there in the ward every morning for the whole of my stay in hospital; I am sure she was not meant to be on duty every day, but there she was, without fail. She brushed my hair until it shone, plaited it into pigtails, and tied it with clean white tape. There was no ribbon to tie it with, but she always managed to find some clean, white tape. She often spent a long time sitting by my bed talking to me, and rolling bandages across her ample bosom. No bandage was ever thrown away - all of them were washed, sterilised, and rolled ready to be used again.

If she thought we needed cheering up, she would walk the length of the ward with a plant pot, or a vase of flowers, balanced on her bosom. Hers was the largest bosom I had ever seen, and the sight of dear, stern faced Nurse Turner striding down the ward, and doing a balancing act at the same time was enough to make anyone feel better no matter how ill, or down in the dumps they might be. The plants and flowers were all taken out of the wards at night, and brought back in again the following morning. I expect this little time of tomfoolery helped to lessen the tedium of that daily task. The staff worked very hard to keep us all as cheerful as possible, one never heard any of them complain about long hours or short rations.

It was generally agreed amongst the medical staff that I would never walk again. Well, I was not having any of that nonsense! So I said,

"I will jolly well walk again, - and by next Easter. I'll be walking by next Easter, I promise."

And walk I did! It took me about half an hour to do a few yards, but I DID IT, and I was very pleased with myself. All the hospital staff, the ones who could leave their posts that is, came running to the ward as soon as they heard the good news. One of the Doctors lifted me as high as he could in the air and threw me onto the bed, amid loud cheers and applause. I was exhausted but ecstatic, I had done it, and the odds were beaten.

Towards the end of my stay in hospital the gym mistress from my new school was brought into the ward, suffering with rheumatic fever. By this time I had learned to 'cope' with a wheelchair, much to the chagrin of the staff and the other patients, whom I narrowly missed more often than I passed them by safely!

Any-way, the gym mistress was pleased to see me, in the wheelchair or out of it. I was shown how I could help to lower her soaring temperature by sponging her down with cold water as often as possible. I spent most of my days trying to make her as comfortable as I could, remembering Mrs Turner's kindness to me, and how much had been done to help me when I was immobile.

Despite the fact that I had only been at my new school a short time before being taken ill, and therefore none of the girls knew me very well, they were asked to write to me and tell me what was happening at school, and in their lives. These letters were usually brought in by one of the teachers, but sometimes some of the children would be allowed into the ward, which created much amusement for them, and the other patients. They were made to wear a mask and a gown, always much too big for them, but this didn't seem to matter, it made them feel very important, and they strutted around the ward pretending to be doctors.

Captain Clifton was admitted into the hospital, having been injured operating the guns in the recreational grounds. He had severe head injuries, and was put into the side ward, just outside the entrance to our main ward.

Great excitement ran through the ward, the nurses and patients alike were agog, - 'A MAN' - a man so close, and here we all were in our night clothes!

After a few weeks he was considered well enough to go out of the hospital and visit his friends in the town.

On one of his subsequent outings he was picked up by the police and detained because he was staggering along the High Street. He was later charged with being drunk and disorderly! He protested and swore that he had not touched a drop of alcohol, but to no avail. It was not until they got him to the police station and took a blood sample, that they found he was telling the truth.

So, why was he 'seemingly' drunk and staggering so? This was the question on all their lips. He told them that he had only recently been injured and was still recovering, and that they must check with the hospital. It was amid great speculation that he was escorted back to the ward by four burly police officers, hanging on tightly to him in case he should try and make a 'get-away'. When the staff assured them that,

"Yes indeed, he is one of our patients." They very reluctantly let go of him and left the ward muttering amongst themselves. I wanted to know every small detail, every word that had been said, over and over again, until I'm sure he must have been exhausted with repeating it all.

When the sirens sounded, heralding yet another air raid, most of the patients were taken down to the bomb shelters. Those of us, who could not be moved, because of being connected to a machine, or something similar, were left in the ward on the top floor of the hospital.

Captain Clifton could have gone to a place of safety with the others, but he chose to stay with me and help me to take my mind off the horror of what was happening just outside the windows - the ones that were left that is. He sat by my bed telling me stories and jokes, or just talking with me, getting us through many terrible nights of bombs and shells.

Sometimes one of the nurses would come up to make sure we were still in the land of the living, but they were kept so busy with casualties being brought in, or with those who were desperately ill, that they had very little time to worry about us. During one of these raids the Captain asked to see my autograph book, he looked through the pages until he came to the last one, and when he saw what Mrs Curtis had written he laughed heartily, and asked for my permission to write on the back cover. He was given it of course, and wrote,

"You are like the old carpet young Curtis, you are beaten again, I'm last in this book!"

When it was decided that it would soon be time for me to go home I was told, "You must learn to swim it will help to strengthen those muscles of yours."

The hospital physiotherapist took me to the baths the next day. She helped me into the water, holding me up and at the same time telling me what to do with my arms and legs. I tried very hard to follow her instructions, but I found it all very, very difficult. If I thought about my arms, my legs went out of control, and vice-versa. None of my extremities would do anything I asked of them. My instructor was always shouting at me to keep my backside down in the water, "You can't learn to swim with your backside sticking up in the air like a hump back whale, get it down, get it down and under the water."

But I could not get it down, or control my body in any of the ways she wanted me to. She pushed me down so hard I was under the water more often than I was going through it. After a few weeks of this, her pushing and shouting, and me crying, she decided that enough was enough. She yelled at me,

"You will never learn to swim, you just don't have a hope in hell of ever learning to swim, I want no more of this, I give up!"

So thankfully I was not taken to the baths again, and neither have I ever learnt to swim. I panic, even if the water just begins to touch my face, I panic. I really have tried very hard to still my fear as I am sure it must be a wonderful feeling to be able to plough through the water. Or just laze about on the surface, but try as I might I have not succeeded.

I left hospital in a wheelchair, and was taken to school in this for a while, but the journey of six miles was much too tiring for my Mother to do every day.

As there was no other way of getting there, the wheelchair wouldn't been allowed on the bus, I did not go again, and so I had no further education.

GETTING THE MESSAGE

One day in my seventeenth year, I was singing the song 'He's just my Bill' over and over, and crying bitterly. I did not know why I was crying - I certainly had no reason to do so.

Why was that song going round and round in my head? I didn't even like the darned song, but, like a record stuck in the jukebox, it went on and on, round and round. I had met a 'Bill' three years earlier when I was first working at Marks and Spencers as a shop assistant. As soon as I was fourteen and had recovered sufficiently, I was put to work there.

Bill was in the Air Force and he and his friends came into the store whenever they were home on leave. They said it was so that they could go to the cafe at the far end of the ground floor. We girls were sure the main reason they came in was to chat us up. And how we loved it. We knew we were quite safe behind our very, wide counters! I was on the stocking counter, but he didn't seem to be at all embarrassed by that - not nearly as much as I was. All those leg's, brazenly pointing their toes to heaven!

On one of Bills visits to the store, he invited me to go home with him and meet his Mother. "My Mother wants to meet you, and has invited you for tea one Saturday afternoon, please say you'll come."

I agreed to go with him the following Saturday. He met me outside the store when I had finished my work for the day. This was the first time I had walked through the town with a man and I felt like a queen, he looked so handsome in his Air Force uniform.

Bill's Mother lived with his stepfather in a small comfy house near Widford Bridge. His stepfather worked for British Rail but was not at home on the day I called. I was given a very warm welcome by Bill's Mother, we had some tea and spent the next few hours happily enough, after which Bill and I went for a walk by the river then he took me home.

Bill was transferred to another base miles away soon after this, and he left promising to write, I heard nothing! I had thought about him often, remembering his Mothers kindness and how proud she was of him; my thoughts of him had always been pleasurable. So why was I feeling like this now? Why was I crying? I could not stop thinking about his Mother and seeing her face, I knew, somehow I knew, I just had to go and see her. Would she still be in that little house by the railway line under the bridge?

At this time I was helping out on a mushroom farm doing whatever needed to be done and was happy enough. I had been raped a few months earlier, on my way home from work at M&S. When I recovered I was not allowed to return to Marks and Spencers. My Mother thought that someone I knew from there must have raped me. I could not tell her that it was one of the men who worked with the horses on the farm, and that he lived right next door to her.

Mrs 'K' (my current employer) was shocked to see me in tears and asked why I was crying. I explained as well as I could, "I don't know why I'm crying but the tears won't stop, I started crying about an hour ago. I keep seeing Bill's Mother's face and can't stop crying. I can't understand it myself so it's very difficult to tell you, or anyone else, what's going on in my head."

Mrs 'K' seemed to understand more clearly than I, she put her arm round my shoulders and said,

"You had better take Anne's bicycle and go to this person she obviously needs you, go along now never mind the clearing up, that can be done any time."

I rode the six miles to Widford, steering the bicycle with one hand and wiping the tears away with the other, still with that song going over and over through my mind. "He's just my Bill an ordinary guy, he hasn't got a thing that I can boast about" Etc, etc.

When I arrived at the house, a stranger opened the door. I thought Bill's Mother must have moved, or worse, that something had happened to her. That would partly explain the 'doomsday' feeling I had been trying to fend off since that morning. Not ever having been told Bill's stepfather's surname I could not ask for his Mother by her surname so I stammered,

"I would like to see the lady who lives here please."

The stranger answered, "You can't see her now. No, you can't come in here today." She was about to go back into the house and tried to shut the door in my face, but Bill's mum had heard my voice and stopped her closing the door. She called to me from somewhere inside the house.

"Come in, please come in, I do want to see you."

I went in, not knowing what to expect and found her sitting by the fire, in tears. I ran across the room and took her in my arms; her whole body was shaking with heartrending, uncontrollable sobs.

Even though I was not much more than a child; it didn't seem at all strange to be holding a middle-aged woman, like a mother cradling her baby. How long we sat there I do not know; I did not know why she was crying and it did not seem necessary to ask. I just knew that she must be allowed to cry as much as she needed. The woman who had answered the door made us a cup of tea, and then she must have left the house, because somehow we were alone together Bill's Mother and I.

Much later that evening Bill's Mother told me that her husband had been killed earlier that day (at precisely the time I had started crying) whilst working on the railway lines near Whitham. I felt utterly help-less. I did not know what to do with this middle-aged stranger. I had not known her husband and had met her just the once when Bill and I had gone to the house for tea three years earlier, she asked me to stay, so I did. We sat through the night, there didn't seem much that I could do except let her cry, and make her a cup of tea when she needed it. We talked about everything and nothing and looked through the photograph albums, which I thought, I hoped, would help her through those tears. I left the next morning and cycled back to Baddow Park to finish that which I had left so abruptly the day before.

So, why was I chosen to be there for her? I did not know. As I have said, I had met her just the once before that day, and had never met her husband. At the time I did not question 'who' or 'what' had sent me to her, I just followed my feelings naturally.

I had forgotten all about Bill's Mother and the death of his stepfather, until I began writing this book, when the whole remarkable episode came flooding back. I have questioned it since, and can only conclude that her need came winging through the barriers of time and space and found a willing soul. Luckily there was also a natural sensitive in the form of Mrs K, in the right place at the right time. Thanks Mrs K.

MY FIRST HOME CIRCLE

Now we need to go back to where this book began. I was married with two daughters and attending the local Congregational Church until that eventful Thursday evening in the back sitting room of the Ministers house.

It was soon after that Thursday that I met Mr Stoneman. He came to tune the piano, and we became firm friends. He was the first person who had talked with me about Spiritual matters; I was very ignorant of such things.

He talked as he worked, and lent me many books on the subject of Spiritualism of which I understood very little. Those books made it all sound very spooky to me. It had still not occurred to me that I was a 'channel' being used by the Spirit world. He also introduced me to my first Home Circle. A friend of his in Sevenoaks held a regular weekly circle in her home. He gave me the friends telephone number, and said that I should call her. I rang her; not knowing what to expect, and was invited to join the group the following week.

When I arrived, there were about ten people of all ages standing around and chatting in the ground floor sitting room. After a while, we went to an upstairs room where we were invited to sit in a circle and hold hands. All the lights in the room were dimmed, and soft music was coming from somewhere.

At some time during the next hour, I found myself on my knees in front of a complete stranger, with my hands on his legs. I had no idea what I was doing there. My hands were making passing movements over his legs, I felt very silly and a touch embarrassed but there was nothing I could do about it. This went on for some minutes, and then I found myself back in my chair.

At the time, it seemed like something that had to be done, something I was being told to do, and I just got on with it. I had gone over to him AND back to my chair, ON MY KNEES, without falling over anyone else's legs, even though the room was in darkness, and it was impossible to see a thing! I had no idea whose legs had been on the receiving end of the 'treatment.'

After the meeting, a man came up to me and asked, "What did you think you were doing on your knees, with your hands on my legs?"

"I don't know. I'm very sorry, I don't know what happened, I just had to come over to you and do those things, I didn't seem to have any control over what was happening." I stammered.

"You know that I have ulcerated legs?"

"No, No, I didn't. Oh dear, I'm so sorry, this is all so very embarrassing for me."

"Well, I have, and they have been open and suppurating for years, and refusing to heal. I am out of pain now for the first time in months. Thank you, Thank you very much."

"But, why are you saying 'thank-you' to me? What did I do, other than kneel in front of you and pass my hands over your legs?" I was squirming at the thought of what I had done.

"Don't you know? You gave me some healing."

"Oh did I? Oh, well then that's good. Isn't it?"

By this time, the others had gathered round, all wanting to know how he was. Obviously they were all aware of what had happened, being regular members of The Circle, and were wanting to hear from him how he felt. I just wanted to go home. I did not feel that the ritual and ceremony were necessarily right for me, and I did not go again.

The people there had also been asking for help for a young boy with a tumour in his head, and who was on the danger list in hospital. The woman in whose home we were, and the one who ran the home Circle had been visiting him in the hospital, he had improved, but his condition was still very worrying.

I heard later from Mr. Stoneman that both of them had been healed that night. The boy suddenly took the path of life instead of death, and the man with the ulcerated legs had no more trouble. I still had no idea how miraculous these things seemed to others. To me, there was nothing strange about knowing what to do, or anything spiritual about it. I was just being me, doing what there was to be done.

I had moved to London, and on a cold November day many years later, I was walking past the Albert Hall looking at the posters displayed outside. My attention was caught by one advertising the Spiritualist Remembrance Service, which was to be held the following day. I bought a ticket for a seat in the stalls, feeling very pleased with myself for being in time to buy one of the only two remaining tickets.

The following evening I was shown to my seat just as the lights were being dimmed for the beginning of the service. After a while I looked around, and saw that every seat in the hall, except for the one on my left, was taken. The hall was full. As I glanced to my right hand side, I saw to my amazement that my neighbour was none other than Mr Stoneman. I had not heard of or from, him for at least ten years! I bought my ticket yesterday, one of the last two left, and now I find that out of all the seats in the Albert Hall I was in the one next to my old friend. I puzzled over this extraordinary coincidence during the first half of the evening, thinking there must be a reason for it.

When the lights came on for the interval I saw that Mr.Stoneman's wife was seated on the other side of him and we chatted for a while, until they went off to find a cup of tea. I had a strange feeling that Mrs. Stoneman suspected that this meeting was not a pure 'coincidence' but it certainly was. No one could have been more surprised than I was to see both Mr and Mrs Stoneman sitting right there next to me. They did not return to their seats after the interval, and I have not seen either of them since.

So was there a reason? I cannot believe that it was just coincidence - how many seats are there in the Albert Hall? For me to have been given the one right next to Mr and Mrs Stoneman, and at the last minute, surely must have been more than pure coincidence. Maybe someone out there can work out the chances of such a thing happening. I imagine it's more than 50 million to 1

But IF there was a reason, why was it not made clear? Or was I just too obtuse to see it?

AUTOMATIC WRITINGS AND DRAWINGS BEGIN.

My younger daughter, Michelle, became very feverish a few weeks after having an operation to remove her tonsils. I recognised the smell, because of my own childhood experience when my gym teacher had been brought into hospital, and I was sure that she had rheumatic fever.

Rheumatic fever, like all illnesses, has its own particular smell, and I know that there is a herb, bearing the same smell, which will cure it: I discovered this living in the country. I also saw that if there is something in nature to harm, there is always an antidote quite close by for example, where there are stinging nettles, there will be dock leaves growing somewhere nearby. The dock leaf is an antidote, if you are stung by nettles, just rub the sting, or wrap the affected part in the leaves, and hey presto no more pain.

Treating illness through the use of herbs has been a fact of life since the beginning of time. Later in my own life this knowledge of herbs and natural remedies was to become very important for me, enabling me to help those people who have been given little or no hope by the medical profession of ever being cured. One does not cure by subduing symptoms with drugs; one simply disguises the cause.

"Find the cause, and you have the cure." is my motto.

However, returning to Michelle, the doctors said, "Of course it's just the measles." Then, after some consideration, "No it's Scarlet fever." Eventually it was decided that, yes indeed, she did have rheumatic fever, and she was taken to hospital in Sevenoaks.

We had arranged as a family to go to Camber, where we had a caravan, for our summer holiday. My husband took Nessa (Vanessa), as he said he badly needed a holiday and did not want to disappoint her, and I stayed at home so that I could visit Michelle each day, this meant I was alone in the house.

One night I was sitting up in bed writing letters, and had just finished writing one to my husband and Nessa in Camber. I lay back on the pillows thinking about them and wondering what they were doing. The pen was resting on the paper I had begun to nod off when, the pen began to move across the paper on its own.

At first, I was so astounded that I could do nothing but watch the letters forming on the page, dozens of letters, but no words that I could make out as there were no spaces between the letters. On and on went the pen, with me getting more and more nervous until I could stand it no longer. I threw the pen and the paper across the room, leapt out of bed, turned all the light's on, and locked all the doors. I don't know what good I thought that would do, I then went back to bed and said the Lord's Prayer until the sun crept over the sill and I felt safe.

I left the pen and paper where they were for two days, afraid to pick them up and look at whatever might be there. Eventually, I convinced myself I must have fallen asleep and dreamed the whole thing. "Of course, a pen can't move on its own - how ridiculous!" I marched upstairs and picked up the paper.

I had not been dreaming; there were the letters, scrawling along the pages at first and then further down the page settling down, still strange, no spaces but much more even. I sat for a long time unscrambling the letters and found words; words about my husband, and his family. Telling me of things that had happened to him and them, long before we had met, none of had been mentioned by him, probably because they were too painful for him to talk about.

There was no way of knowing if any of what had been written was true without asking him, and he was not due back from Camber for weeks. I picked up the pen and started to write a letter to John and Nessa - and immediately the pen took off again, starting as before, letters together. No separation, but after a few lines beginning to make words and sentences. As the pen moved over the paper, I began to sense, incredulous at first that this writing was very like his mother's hand. After two or three more attempts at writing to him, all with the same results, - I picked up the pen, IT went off on its own. I gave up trying to write to him and marched up the road to the Post Office from where I sent a telegram telling John I would be there the next day.

I visited Michelle and told her I had to see Daddy and Nessa and that I would be back the next evening. I hated not seeing her for the day, but I had to know if he also saw what had been written as his mother's writing. When I arrived I was so impatient for him to see the writing that I could hardly wait to hear how they were and what had been happening to them.

At length he asked me "What are you doing here? Why aren't you with Michelle?"

Saying nothing, I gave him just one page of the writings. He looked, read the page and jumped up from the chair he'd been sitting on as though some one had stuck a pin in him! "But this is Ma's writing. I didn't know she had told you about this. When did she write this to you? You didn't show me."

"Last night."

"Don't be stupid, Ma died a year ago."

"That was written last night."

"I think being on your own has made you lose your mind. You had better see someone, and quickly."

"But I can prove those words were written last night. Let's ask Ma a question and we'll get an answer, I'm sure we will."

"Oh, don't be so damned silly!"

"All right, I'll ask." I wrote the question. "Ma, is there anything you want your son to know?"

The answer came quick as a flash, written as before in Ma's hand. "Tell John we know all about Anne."

"Well, well what does it say?" John asked with a cynical smile playing round his lips.

I showed him the paper. His face went a strange shade of grey, he seemed to have difficulty breathing and fell onto the bed with a thump. After a few seconds he visibly shook himself, pulled himself together and said, "It is all a load of nonsense I know no one called Anne. You had better stop this or you'll go mad."

I knew then that what had been written was right, otherwise my husband would not have been so upset. I went home a wiser but much sadder girl.

It was soon after this that the drawings started coming through. Michelle was fit and back home again and John and Ness had returned from Camber, so things were back to normal.

I had never been able to draw, and at first it was quite difficult for me to understand what was happening to me. I was trying to control the drawings emerging from under the pencil, I thought I knew what they were going to be. Well you would wouldn't you? The pencil is in your hand, so you must be doing the drawing right? Wrong.

Once I got my head round this frightening fact, I gradually learned to relax and allow the pencil and my hand to be guided by the strange force which seemed to control both my hand and arm, and the drawing became much easier. I soon learned to recognise the feeling and know when I had to pick up a pencil, I don't know how I knew, I just knew that my arm felt somehow different, as though some sort of power was surging through it. This only ever affected my right arm and hand - never the left one. When this happened, I just had to stop what I was doing and sit down ready to start a drawing!

My husband was amazed at these drawings. He had trained as a technical draughtsman and was now working on nuclear warheads, he knew I had never been able to draw a straight line without help. When he saw the first drawing taking shape, he said,

"My goodness girl, I didn't know you could draw like that, that's very good."

"I still can't draw like that, it isn't me; someone else is doing it."

He shook his head, gave me a very strange look and went into the other room. Although he was obviously uncertain about what was happening with the drawings, even he began to show an interest when I started to draw people neither of us knew. Many faces were drawn over the next few months. Sometimes the same face would be drawn from different angles, over and over again; we knew none of these people at the time but strange as it seems, I have since met all of them. I'm sure it was necessary for me to recognise them from the drawings, and know them before I knew them. What puzzled me more was the fact that they also recognised and acknowledged me, a complete stranger.

An incident occurring around this time reassured me that I was not alone in this recognition of 'strangers.'

My friend, Babs, and I had been invited to visit a small village in Kent, owned and run by a group of people known as 'The Seekers'. The group had been formed in the earlier part of this century by a Mr. Simpson who was a trance medium. His Spirit guide a Doctor Lascelles spoke through him and instructed the group to build a village for the purpose of praising God and healing the sick.

This had been done and the village was now flourishing. Babs and I had been invited to the opening ceremony of a new conference hall. The person who was welcoming the guests as they arrived fell into my arms saying,

"How wonderful to see you again. How are you? It's so long since we met."

Once we were inside the hall and out of earshot, Babs said to me, "Who is that? I didn't know you had any friends here."

I had to admit that I did not know who the woman was, but that I knew her well in Spirit. I tried to explain what I meant, "You know the sort of feeling you get when you see someone for the first time and yet, you know you know them so well?"

Babs said, "Yes, I know, that does happen sometimes, it's the strangest feeling and yet you know it's right."

At various times during the day I looked up to see the 'greeter' glancing my way with a puzzled look on her face, then at the end of the day she was waiting for us when we came out, she approached me saying,

"We haven't met have we? Yet I feel I know you so well, why is that do you think?"

I smiled and said "Perhaps we work together in sleep-state. I know you because I've drawn you dozens of times."

"Really?" she said, giving me a very strange look.

"Yes, but I have always put you in Nun's habit."

"Oh, that's not surprising my dear, I was a Nun for twenty years."

We became very good friends, and I visited 'The Seekers' often over the next few years. As you will read later on in this book, when my daughter died I planted a rose tree in the remembrance garden there.

GLYN'S HELPERS FIND THEIR WAY HOME.

In the spring of 1963 my husband had a letter from Glyn Collins, an acquaintance of his from the years before we met, telling him that he was now living on a farm in Zennor in Cornwall. He wrote that he would like it if we, as a family, could go and spend the spring with him and his new wife, Margaret. My husband told me that before Glyn had moved to Zennor he had been a reasonably successful artist living in Earls Court, but since he had moved to Cornwall he had done very little work except for painting some small cards for the tourists when he needed extra cash.

He was living on National Assistance, which he spent as soon as he received it in the nearest pub. My husband's reaction to the letter was immediate.

"Good heavens, I hardly know the man. Of course we will not go."

I knew we had to go. Why we had to go I did not know. I just knew that we must. After a week or so of telling John how good it would be for the children, and how much the sea air helped with sinus troubles, from which he suffered, he agreed that we could go.

We drove down on the Sunday a few weeks later, and by the time we arrived in Cornwall John (my husband) was in the foulest of moods. The farmhouse where Glyn and Margaret were staying was at the end of a long, very badly maintained cart track, and John was very concerned for his car. The car was a low slung Healey Tickford so the exhaust and the petrol tanks were constantly hitting the ground. This car was his pride and joy, and a rare and valuable possession. It had taken John years to find that particular model and it was more important to him than anything or anyone, including me. Blue and sleek, fast and unique, it played the major role in his life, everything else coming a very poor second. The pounding it had received while being driven the final half a mile down the farm track had distressed John as much as it had the poor car.

We were met by Margaret who offered us some supper. When we had eaten, it was time to put the children to bed. Margaret showed us to our rooms and I asked her "Where's Glyn? Isn't he here?"

"No, he's in the pub, he'll probably be there until it closes and then come home. You had better prepare yourselves as he'll more than likely be drunk."

"Oh dear, does this happen very often? I hope it has nothing to do with our arrival."

"No, it really has nothing to do with you. In fact I'm hoping that your being here will help a bit, and he won't want to go to the pub so often."

John gave me one of those 'If looks could kill, you'd be dead on the spot.' looks - which clearly meant that if it hadn't been a twelve hour drive back to Sevenoaks he would have left there and then!

Glyn came back to the house around eleven and sure enough he was drunk, very, very, drunk, and smelled of cow's dung. He had fallen over as he came rolling back across the fields from the pub, and had obviously found some fresh cow's dung to roll in. Now, even I was beginning to think that perhaps John was right and we should not have come at all.

However, the next two days were spent happily enough exploring the surrounding countryside with Glyn and Margaret, and we all retired to bed on the Tuesday night happy and totally relaxed - Glyn did not seem to have missed his nightly sessions at 'The Mermaid Inn' too much.

We were drifting into sleep when I was rudely brought back to full consciousness by something moving in front of my face; it was a large American flag, fluttering back and forth before my eyes. This disappeared after a while, and in its place I 'saw' a cottage with an aeroplane resting on the back of the roof. There was no sign of there having been a crash, no wreckage, no feeling of death or terror, nothing but a wonderful sense of peace. The aeroplane was double winged and had propellers, I knew in my heart that this plane was a passenger carrying aircraft and not a private one, so I wondered why there were no people about.

Over to the left of this scene unfolding in front of my eyes was a line of tall plane trees, all of the surrounding countryside could be seen quite clearly, a lane leading from the road to the cottage; and the hedges bordering this lane. The atmosphere was one of quiet serenity.

Then, the silence was broken by voices, indistinct voices, I tried to hear what was being said but could not. Then, one voice became very clear and I heard the words, "It's all right now we've found our way, we can go now. We're going on - thank you for all your help, thank you, goodbye."

The whole scene was suffused with brilliant light and gradually faded from my sight leaving me mystified but untroubled because the message had clearly been that 'it is all right now.'

John was almost asleep by this time but I needed to tell him what I had seen. He listened impatiently - he was quite used to my knowing about things before they occurred so he simply shrugged his shoulders and said, "It sounds as though there has been an air crash in America. You'll just have to make allowances for the time difference, now let's get some sleep shall we?"

Early the following morning I threw on my blue knitted dress to cover my nakedness and crept down to the kitchen, - (isn't it strange how I still hate making a noise, especially in someone else's house?) I wanted to make some tea for John and myself before the rest of the household stirred. I was amazed to see that Glyn was already up and about! He was standing by an open window mixing something in a pot. His back was turned to the stairs I had just crept down. I saw that there was a large, new canvas stretched and on the easel. I tried to slip into the kitchen behind the stairs without his seeing me, but I was not careful or quick enough, he turned, saw me, and said

"Good, good you're up early, come and sit down here in this chair I'm going to paint you today."

"Oh, but you can't, I have to make the tea for John and me and anyway I'm not dressed. John's waiting for his tea and he'll be furious if he doesn't get it soon." I stammered.

"Never mind about the damned tea. We don't have time to mess about making tea; there's work to be done. Just do as you are told and sit." So I SAT!

John came wandering down the stairs bleary eyed about half an hour later, wanting to know what had happened to the tea.

"Where's my tea, what have you been up to all this time? Why are you sitting there? You're supposed to be bringing me some tea."

I started to rise from the chair but Glyn came over and gently pushed me down into the chair again saying,

"Stay just where you are, I need you to be there. Let him get his own tea, if he needs it so much he can get it himself."

He turned to John, who was standing open mouthed at this insolence and said,

"And, when you've had your tea you will take Margaret and the girls and do a disappearing trick for the rest of the day, don't come back here until tonight, do you understand? I don't want to see any of you until it's quite dark."

John was definitely not amused. He did not like being told what to do at the best of times, and he always took great pains to work out what he would do next and how he would do it.

He never did anything without thinking about it and planning for a long time.

But, off they all went an hour or so later looking very bemused. The children were wondering why they had to go out so early and without 'Mummy'.

"Why isn't Mummy coming? Why is Mummy sitting there? What is Uncle Glyn doing with our Mummy?"

These and many other questions came floating back to me as they were walking away up the lane to who knew where. I wanted run out and reassure them but knew that Margaret would be able to explain. I sat, and Glyn painted until eleven. I was thinking,

'If I don't have something to drink soon I'll die of thirst,' when Glyn put down his brush and said,

"Right, now we can have that a cup of coffee." I very rarely drink coffee but I was so thirsty I heard myself saying.

"Wonderful! That's just what I need."

While we were drinking our coffee I heard again the echo of the young man's voice of last night,

"We're going now, Thank you, thank you so much, goodbye."

I knew I had to tell Glyn about my experience of the previous night. He listened in absolute silence becoming more pale with each detail, until I came to the end of the story, by which time he had collapsed into the nearest armchair and I was worried in case he was about to die, his face was ashen.

"Can I get you something? What is it? Are you all right?"

Glyn slowly shook his head and said,

"No, I don't need anything, by God you are psychic aren't you, - you know that I was born and brought up in America don't you?"

"No, no I didn't know. I know nothing about you or your life."

"Well, I was! And that is why you saw the Stars and Stripes last night."

"But the plane trees, the aeroplane, the voices - what about all of them, what did they have to do with anything?"

"Well, that is the incredible part really. You see, I'd never painted or even felt the urge to pick up a brush or pencil until I rented a little cottage in Shoreham, a small village in Kent. I felt - oh yes, from the minute I moved in - I felt that I just had to paint, I knew I must get paints, canvasses, brushes, everything an artist needs, it was as if I was possessed. I could not understand what was happening to me.

The paintings that were done were all very good, but - there were so many different styles, changing sometimes hour by hour, so I would be working on one and then have to go and do some more work on another completely different one.

Working frantically as though there were no tomorrow. After I had been living there for some time I found out that before I had moved into the cottage a 'plane had crashed, not on the cottage, but in a field behind the cottage.

There is a memorial there to mark the spot. The 'plane was exactly as you saw it, a double-winged passenger plane coming back from an art exhibition in Paris, that is why you saw the plane trees - the passengers were all art students who had been the cream of the art colleges in this country! The trip was a prize for them. They were all killed in the crash.

Years later I left the cottage and moved to London, but even there I seemed to be 'haunted' do you know what I mean? Silly question, of course you do or you wouldn't be here, would you?"

I nodded, shivering a little as I began to understand the enormity of what had happened. I saw now that I was needed here for the drama to unfold, without me there would not have been enough power.

So that's why I knew we had to come here for the spring holidays. Why I had also felt 'haunted', obsessed with the knowledge that we must go to Zennor. I came, to share in, to make possible, this remarkable ending of an amazing story.

Glyn continued, "I thought that by moving down here I might find some peace, and would feel free to try MY hand at painting or whatever else there was to do. But as you have seen, I have done very little - I didn't want to be used by anyone any more, dead or alive. I was afraid to start a painting in case one of them came and took over again."

"So why did you decide to get everything ready to paint me today?" I asked.

"Because last night I too heard that voice saying they were going, and I wanted to see if I could work without their help. I have been up most of the night getting the canvas stretched and ready, and mixing the paints. This all seems so incredible. I really didn't know if it was my imagination last night or what it was, until you told me of your experience. Now I know that it really is so and I am free we must get back to work, are you ready?"

Glyn worked all through that day and the next few days as long as there was light to see by. The finished portrait was one of the most beautiful paintings I have ever seen.

He could not put a top on my head, try as he might. I later found out that this was because he was seeing me in a 'psychic way' and the top of my head was open to show my continued contact with the source of knowledge and truth.

In the painting my arms were folded across my middle and on my right were blues, greens, pinks and gold, all apparently flowing into the top of my head my arms seeming to hold and capture them in my body. These are the colours often associated with psychic work, healing spiritual colours.

To my left were the material colours, reds, oranges, dark blues, and browns, all just swirling around, going nowhere.

The whole experience showed me how important it is to listen to our intuitions and be guided by them.

If I had not insisted on going to Zennor, Glyn would probably have gone on drinking every night in the Mermaid pub and avoiding his painting. He certainly would not have been in a fit state to hear the voice and be released to get on with his work. Two or three more paintings were done before John decided it was time we went home; Glyn was working in earnest again.

A few months later, he sent us this notice of an exhibition of his paintings at Jacques Seligmans Galleries in New York. They had bought the first painting he did of me, and this gave him enough money to go on painting.

I have not heard of him since. He was talking of changing his name. Maybe he did. That would explain why I have not seen 'Glyn Collins' mentioned anywhere in the art world honours list.

I hope he is still painting out there somewhere. If you are there Glyn please give me a call.

There is always a reason for everything that happens to us, and in the end the reason is always a good one. Whatever happens, something good comes from it and we can always look back and say,

"If that hadn't happened I wouldn't be here now." or "I would not have met so and so."

I have found so many times that what is seemingly disastrous, turns out to be God-sent for a very good reason. As G.K. Chesterton said

"A nuisance is an adventure wrongly conceived."

Kind regards to both,
Glyn

GLYN COLLINS
PAINTINGS

NATIVITY, a triptych 1. Caprice 2.
Nude 3. Bijou and Wickedness 4.
. . a la Japonaise 5. THE MIRACLE
. . from the Holy Shroud at Turin 6.
Keening Women 7. The Parasol 8.
Intimacy 9. Femme en Rouge 10.
On the Balcony . . . Gabrielle D'Estree
et sa Soeur? 11. Vainglory 12.
Director of the Choir 13. Midi 14.

LONDON LANDSCAPES
Winters Walk 15.
Holland Walk 16.
Elm at Coombe 17.
Summer's Beech 18.

Permandor Ball 19. Crystal Vase 20.
The Little Venetian, Lord Kinross 21.
' L'ILE ST LOUIS 22.

APRIL 14 ✦ APRIL 28

CONTEMPORARY AMERICAN DEPARTMENT
JACQUES SELIGMANN GALLERIES
5 East 57th Street   NEW YORK 22

ANOTHER DRAWING COMES TO LIFE.

An apparently disastrous event happened when I was trying to raise money to buy a house in Tunbridge Wells to open as a hostel for mothers and babies. I had been working very hard night and day, visiting bank managers, health people, and writing letters to others who might be able to help with funds. That morning, I had extracted a promise from one bank manager that if I raised £10,000 he would lend us double that amount. I was overjoyed and determined to work twice as hard to raise the £10,000.

I began to get searing pains in my chest and left arm. The doctor was called and I was sent to hospital. "Coronary Thrombosis." they said, "bed for you, my girl."

I was lying there in that hospital bed, railing against heaven and God for allowing this to happen. "You know how much work I have to do, how could you do this to me?"

I felt someone looking at me, looked up, and there standing in the doorway between the small ward I was in and the larger one, was a woman looking at me very intently.

I realised with a shock that this was one of the people I had drawn many times in that period of 1963. I knew that face so well, she could have been my sister, I recognised every line.

Her portraits had always had the initials C.B. on them. None of the others had been signed and I was always faintly puzzled by this. She came across to my bed and asked,

"May I come and talk to you?"

I answered, "Yes, yes of course you can. Please, please come and sit on my bed."

I gave her a cigarette and had one myself, strictly against the rules of course, but I was so shaken I felt I needed one. To see another of my drawings in the flesh was quite a shock. Now I had to know, were her initials C.B? We chatted for a while and I asked her,

"Why are you here?"

She told me "I had a child, and the child died, so they brought me up here to recover, away from the other mothers and babies." She talked of her home and family and told me her name was Mrs. Charlie Brown.[1] (So the initials were right.) She said how much she missed her family and how she so badly wanted to be at home with them.

"I hate being here, no one understands who I am, or what I need, but I felt you would. That's why I needed to come and talk to you."

[1] <u>not</u> real name

She told me how upset she had been when she lost the baby, and I tried to comfort her. Having lost children of my own I felt I knew what she was going through. Later, when she had returned to her own part of the ward, the Staff Nurse came and asked me, "What have you two been talking about?"

I did not think it any of her business and said so. She insisted on knowing, so I told her that the woman had talked to me about losing her child, and how upset she had been.

The nurse tossed her head and said sourly. "That was all ten years ago. She is in here now to dry out."

I was not at all sure what she meant by 'dry out'.

Sometimes, after this, when she came to talk to me, the woman would be totally coherent. At other times, thinking she was at home she wandered around asking any one that would listen,

"Where's Shirley, why won't you tell me, where's Shirley?"

Shirley was Mrs C.B.'s, older daughter and was at home with her, Mrs. C.B.'s, husband. The other patients and staff had no patience with her and would say to her,

"Don't be so stupid. You are in hospital. Shirley isn't here."

She did not understand and would then became very angry, throwing anything within her reach. If I was there, I tried to give her a simple answer to what she thought was a perfectly simple question. I would say something like,

"Shirley has gone shopping and she'll be back in a minute."

She would be quite satisfied with that, and wander off and get on with something else.

One evening, I was lying on my bed watching through the doorway connecting the wards, waiting in case I might have a visitor.

Mrs. C.B. had two visitors; Mr C B. and Shirley. Mr C B. sat on the right hand side of her bed, her daughter, Shirley, on the side nearest me.

Her husband gave her a packet of cigarettes; she thanked him and put them on the top of the locker on the side of the bed where her husband was sitting.

She then turned to her right to talk to her daughter. As she did so, her husband picked up the cigarettes and put them back in his pocket.

A while later she turned to talk to him, - leaned over to pick up the cigarettes, found that they were no longer there, and asked,

"Where are my cigarettes?"

"What cigarettes?"

"The ones you gave me."

"But I didn't give you any cigarettes."

"You did, you did, I put them there on the locker. There, that's where I put them." she said, banging her fist on the locker where she had put them, and where I had seen her put them.

"You're crazy. I didn't bring you any cigarettes. You are going mad, imagining things, I warned you about this, it's one of the first signs of madness."

"I am not mad. You did, you did give me a pack of cigarettes." And saying this she began to hit out at him screaming all the time. "You did, you did. I put them on the locker. You did give me some cigarettes."

By this time, the other patients were getting very upset. Nurses rushed in and grabbed Mrs C B. I got myself into my wheelchair and reached the Sister's office just as they were about to close the door, having taken the woman, Mrs. C.B., her husband and her daughter Shirley inside. I told them that she had been given a packet of cigarettes and they had been taken. I had seen the whole thing from my bed. She was shouting at me "Don't let them do it, Sally, don't let them do it. They are trying to put me away. You know what they are doing, that's why you're here, do something."

The Staff Nurse was by this time tying her into a straight jacket, and she was bundled into a cot in the side ward. They gave her an injection, although I tried hard to stop them, knowing she could be calmed down if someone would just talk to her, but to no avail. Her husband and daughter were sent home, and the Sister took me into her office and explained how she saw the situation.

"It's like this," she said "we do know what has been going on but it's to late now to do any thing about it. The woman, Mrs C.B, started drinking after she lost her child, and her husband encouraged her, as it seemed to help at first. He then realised that when she was 'in drink' he could get away with so many things, including spending money like water. Mrs C.B. is a very wealthy woman, and if she is certified he collects everything. I'm afraid she has now indulged in so much drink that she has destroyed her liver and her nervous system is a wreck, her brain is nigh on useless. She will never be mentally fit again."

The next morning she was gone. By the time I woke up they had taken her to Oakwood Mental Hospital so; her husband had got his way.

Did I fail? Was I meant to do more to help her, or was it just necessary for me to be there to answer her questions and help when I could?

I do not know. I have wondered many times what I was meant to do, if any thing. Sometimes it seems that we appear to 'fail' because we misinterpret the message our intuition, or 'Spirit', gives us. A couple of months after I had been discharged from the hospital, this truth was brought home to me very strongly, and very sadly.

MICHELLE'S KITTEN.

Michelle, my youngest child had a kitten, which was longhaired and very beautiful hence, Michelle's name for her - Beauty. Beauty became very ill; she could not eat, and had great difficulty breathing when she tried to lie down. We called the in Vet who gave her an injection, and said we should try and feed her with warm milk and brandy through a dropper. If she would take it, she might survive. If not, there was not a thing that could be done for her.

Later that night, having comforted the children as best I could, I was sitting in the armchair with the kitten, holding her up so that she could sleep. The family was all in bed and we, Beauty and I, were in the dining room by the fire, which burned continuously to provide the family with hot water.

As we sat there I 'saw,' (as in a vision,) myself putting her on the chair surrounding her with cushions to keep her upright and telling her that I had to get the breakfast, as the family would be down soon.

Still in my vision, I went into the kitchen to prepare breakfast. When I came back into the dining room a few minutes later, she had put herself on the fire. I pulled her out. She was singed a bit but was all right. So I put her back into the chair and, wagging my finger at her, told her how silly she was and that she must stay there on the chair and must not go near the fire again.

I then went back to the kitchen to continue preparing the breakfast. When I came back next time, she had put herself on the fire again and this time it was too late to save her; she was burned beyond recognition.

All this I 'saw 'as I sat in the comfortable armchair in front of a glowing fire, holding the kitten in my hands. I told myself it was very stupid to imagine such dreadful things, and I tried to put them out of my mind. After a few days she recovered, and was running around happily again. We were all over the moon and enjoyed her playful company.

Three weeks later, as I put my coat on for the trip to Sevenoaks to do the shopping I had the strange feeling that someone was at the back of the house, I opened the back door and found Beauty lying dead on the door-step. I bent down, picked her up, and cradling her in my arms took her to the shed at the bottom of the garden; I laid her gently in a box to wait until the family came home and we could bury her in her favourite spot under the lilac tree.

I now knew what I had been shown that night. I was being told that there was no point in trying to save her life, as she was destined to die quite soon anyway, but in my ignorance I did not interpret this as the message of my 'vision' at the time.

SPIRIT WILL HAVE THEIR WAY.

Messages have come unbidden over the years, wherever I am. If it is necessary for, 'That person over there' to be told something, or warned about a forthcoming event, there is nothing I can do but obey and tell, or warn, that person or persons.

No matter how much I resist, complain, or protest that I will look ridiculous going up to strangers and telling them some tale; I am still not allowed to get away without doing what 'The Management' requires of me, they always win!

"Well," you say, "where does free will come into that scenario?" I know what you mean, I've asked myself that question many times and I'm not surprised that you are wondering too. I will try to show how I have learned over the years to accept the unexplainable!

My way's are. To first search diligently for a rational explanation to phenomenon, and then, if there is still no answer, to accept that there are greater things etc. I can not, as some do, blindly believe that each time a light goes out as I walk by, that it must be because Spirit is around. Or if a bottle suddenly comes flying across the room, that Spirit must be angry with me! Most of the time there is a completely rational explanation to these phenomenon, it is very rarely the work of the Almighty.

I had just finished rewriting that last passage - and decided that I would like to listen to some of my favourite music 'Beethovens Missa Solemnis' so I went and put the cassette in the player.

It sounded terrible, so thinking the machine was on the blink, I transferred the tape to the radio cassette player, the same dreadful sound came bursting out. Every apparatus in the house seemed to be to have given up the ghost! I decided to give it one last try on the music centre and it chewed the damn tape up. How's that for instant retribution! I used to wonder why we can see so clearly for others, what they have to do, where to go etc., but find it so very difficult to know for ourselves. I'm sure we could know if we didn't try so hard.

When we worry and concern ourselves with our problems we are really only arguing with our selves, our own conscious mind. We are thereby shutting out the answers, standing in our own light so to speak. We 'shut the top of our head' when we do that. As I mentioned earlier in the book 'Glyn could not put a top on my head' because he was seeing me in a psychic way, the way I am when I am being used/working with Spirit.

When I see people for a clairvoyant reading, I do not want know the pro's and con's, I will never allow anyone to tell me anything or ask any questions before we start a reading. That way I can be open enough to listen to the answers from Spirit, without being influenced by the questions. I can listen to the answers that Spirit KNOW are needed, rather than those the client thinks they WANT to hear, there is a subtle difference. It's only when I allow the ego bit of me to come to the surface that I have difficulties.

The ego surfaced again a while ago, when I had received a letter from a client, which read,

"Dear Selena, I was wondering whether you would be interested in giving a 'demonstration' of your remarkable powers to a small sympathetic group of serious students of the paranormal in Kensington. I was much impressed when I came to you the other day, and have recommended you to many of my friends, including a TV company.

With all good wishes, Yours sincerely, Howard C."

My immediate reaction was, NO, NO, NO; I will not prostitute my gifts by showing off. This is how I always I feel when I'm asked to 'go public.' But, I was persuaded to go to the meeting by well meaning 'friends' who had recognised the address where the meeting was to be held.

I went, reluctantly, but I went, after having consumed a large amount of brandy, given me by these same 'well meaning friends,' and of course the demonstration was a complete fiasco.

Once again the ego bit had surfaced I had wanted to impress these important people. I had been told that this group was most influential in investigating all things to do with the psychic world. Stupid girl that I am, I KNOW when the 'I' becomes important, truth flies out of the window. I have found this to be a fact so often.

I'm sure this is why it is so difficult to prove scientifically that there truly is such a thing as 'communication' with Spirit.

I AM TOLD TO GO HOME.

When 'The Management' find it difficult to make me listen to what is required of me they try all sorts of tricks to get through. During my marriage I travelled from Sevenoaks to London two or three nights a week as I felt I should be doing something to help the dropouts who hung around the main railway stations, sleeping on benches and in the waiting rooms, where it was always reasonably warm. (Until they were thrown out by the station staff) - I walked around talking to them and bought them a cup of tea or some soup when they would accept it. I had a list of hostels and night shelters where they could go for a night's rest and tried to persuade as many as I could to stay in one or other of these places sometimes taking them there myself.

Many of them had no warm clothes and I brought clothes with me which we, as a family no longer needed. The railway police, who had an office on most main stations, called me a 'bloody do-gooder' and told me in no uncertain terms to go home, and mind my own business.

"They only sell the clothes and so get more money for their booze and drugs. You do more harm than good. You are just using your good intentions as a crutch."

My husband also felt that I was being very silly. 'God helps those who help themselves,' was his favourite quotation - I thought, IF I could get just a few of them into a hostel where they could get a bed every night and be well fed they may have a chance to get their lives in some sort of order.

I used to cry myself to sleep every night over one old lady who sat on a bench near platforms 1 and 2 at Victoria Station, day and night. She had been there since the war, waiting for her soldier to come home. Her legs were ulcerated by sleeping with them hanging down all the time, and she would not accept help of any kind.

One night I was in the house alone, crying over her yet again, when a loud voice boomed through the house.

"How long must you go on? When will you understand that you can't help anyone while you are hurting yourself by doing it?"

I convinced myself that I had imagined the whole thing but the voice came again.

"How long must you go on? WHEN will you understand that you can not help while you are hurting yourself?"

I did not understand what was meant at first, but it came to me later that all I was doing with my crying was destroying a bit of myself. I was not helping her, or any one else, in any way.

So I stopped crying, and resisted trying to persuade her to go into a hostel. I sat and talked with her if and when SHE wanted me to. I brought her a bowl of soup or a cup of tea when she would allow it; but I did not cry over her again.

I understand now, IF we can see what to do for the starving people of the world, then we should worry about it and get it done. If we can not see the answer after careful thought, there is no point in wasting our emotions and energies in worrying.

We should say our prayers and ask if there is something we can do, and if there is, to be shown what it is. If we can be of use anywhere we are always shown what to do if we ask and listen.

When we see an old lady carrying a heavy suitcase we KNOW if we should help her. Or, if she needs to prove something to herself, or to someone else, by carrying it on her own.

We know, but how often do we listen? Not often enough I say, speaking for myself!

NEW HOME NEW CHILD

I left my husband because of his violence. My doctor had said, "If you don't leave, there is nothing I can do for you. You will not survive another beating."

No one in my husband's family believed me when I told them of his violence, I knew I would have to leave soon and I wanted them to know why I was going, I tried talking about it with his brother and his wife. My husband John insisted, "It's all in her imagination. Of course I have never laid a finger on her, or the girls."

Most of my teeth had been knocked out by him on Nessa's 11th birthday, I went flying down the stairs spitting broken teeth out on the way down. This meant spending most of the next week at Guy's Hospital having the last of the broken pieces taken out of the gums. He neither inquired how I was, or came to see me whilst I was there. I stayed with him for another four years, being beaten up as often as he felt like it. Usually after he had been drinking Worthington's and Scotch.

I stayed until both his parents had died; I would not have been able to bear it if they had known what he was like toward us. I have wondered since if he would have done those things to anyone else. I have asked myself that question time and time again. Did I create the problem, was there something about me, or my behaviour that made him hate me so much one day, and love me so powerfully a few days later? Was I stupid allowing him to get away with such barbaric treatment for so many years? Of course I was, but really, I didn't think I had a choice. Where would I go with two teenagers, how would we survive?

I wanted to live, and to have another child. I had lost six children, some miscarriages due to his violence, and one burst ectopic pregnancy with another child growing in the womb at the same time, a very rare occurrence.

I desperately wanted to have another baby. Michelle and Nessa were fourteen and fifteen years old and we three had what we called 'Our council of war,' and decided we must leave the family home. But where to go, and how?

My husband had said "If you leave I will make sure you get nothing from me, you'll end up in a council house somewhere. If you make me go I'll stop the mortgage and you'll be thrown out in the street."

I was equally sure that he meant it. I asked my Father to help me, but, "It was jam yesterday, it will be jam again tomorrow, but it's margarine today. Sorry but that's how it is." was his retort. So I knew I would have to do something to make us self-sufficient. I had no idea how we would achieve it. We three had no money of our own and I certainly had no qualifications on paper to enable me to get a well paid job, which I thought was necessary if we were to survive.

One evening in March soon after our decision to move was made, I called in to see a neighbour, Jo, who had become a good friend, and she and I talked about my leaving the family home. A man friend of hers arrived and I stood up to go home, but they pressed me to stay. During the evening, Jo mentioned that I was leaving my husband and that I needed somewhere to live.

Her visitor asked, "How about a ten roomed house on the seafront in Herne Bay?"

"Where is it, what's it like?" I asked, very excited by the prospect of being able to leave my husband, and his violence, sooner than I had dared hope.

"Find me a map Jo, and I'll show you both just where it is." Turning to me he said, "I'm sure you'll love it there."

Maps were brought out and we located the town. I had never heard of the place before that evening. He told me how to get there, what the rent would be and who to see.

"It sounds absolutely right." I said. "When can I see it?"

"Here's the telephone number. Ring tomorrow and speak to a Mr. King."

I telephoned Mr. King the next day and arranged to see the house on the first available date his agent had free. Michelle came to see the house with me. It was not beautiful but it was just what we needed. We agreed to take it on a seven-year lease, starting that day, April 7th. When we left the family home, we took some of the contents, the things we would need to exist, like the girls beds, leaving the house and enough furniture for my husband to live reasonably comfortably.

He kept his word; I never received any money from him. Nothing from the sale of our home, or any of the money his father had left both of us a few months earlier.

For a time, I fostered the young children of students studying at Canterbury University. Michelle went to the local school and Ness stayed on for a while at her boarding school. Later came the opportunity for her to become a 'pinky' (a student nurse) at the Queen Victoria Hospital, in East Grinstead, doing two months in each department of the hospital as a preliminary to a full nursing training. So off she went to do that.

I bought furniture for our new house from auctions and jumble sales. There were so many 'extra' items in auction lots that I bought. After some months, I rented a shop to enable me to sell these. People referred to it as an antique shop, but it was in fact a junk shop. From here I sold the extras that had been thrown in with, say, a table that I wanted. Quite often if one bought a cupboard it would be full of bits and pieces, and sometimes come with a chair as well.

If these things were not needed in the house they all went to the shop to be sold. I had made friends with a couple who had an antique shop, they brought things round to me that they would not sell in their own shop, and I sold these on commission.

My 'shop' had been a builder's merchant's store and there was a large walled yard in front of the long low building that had been the storeroom. Tables that I had for sale were used to display the small pieces of china and silver. Plants in tubs were scattered about outside. Local artists hung their pictures round the walls of the yard and in the shop and it all looked very inviting. The 'shop' walls were lined with hessian, which I bought very cheaply in an auction sale. I also made curtains for the house from this roll of hessian. These curtains looked very good, but it is not to be recommended, Hessian smells really badly. Anyone coming through the front door of the house held their noses until they got used to the smell!

When we had furnished enough of the rooms we let them to five students from Canterbury University. I did breakfasts and evening meals for them.

I also started an, 'alarm call' service, 10/- a month - (50p new money)- seriously undercutting the G.P.O! This worked so well that I decided to 'branch out,' and had leaflets printed offering a speedy delivery service for urgent letters and messages, - two old pence each. Michelle and I must have walked hundreds of miles. We had no transport and everything had to be done in the evenings, after I had closed the shop and cooked the evening meal, and Michelle had worked in school all day and finished her homework.

In this way, we paid the bills and kept things going.

By this time, I was well into my pregnancy and during the student's spring holiday, Michelle and I went to stay with my friend Babs near Tunbridge Wells.

After a week or so my left leg became very inflamed and swollen. The doctor was called in and said that I had developed Thrombophlebitis and must go into hospital. He refused to allow me to go home and insisted that I was to be taken to the nearest hospital, which was in Pembury.

Nessa was doing well with her training at East Grinstead. And, of course, she lived in the students quarters at the hospital.

It was decided that Michelle should go to a local school near the hospital I was in, and stay on with Babs. Another of my friends, Connie,

We offer the following 'Services' ───────

1. Reminders of Important Appointments, Birthdays, Weddings, etc. Birthday Cards and, or Presents sent in your name on correct date.

2. Delivery Service of Minutes, Notices of Meetings, Accounts, Reminders. 2d. each delivery! (No more 4d. stamps.)

3. Early Morning Calls 10/- per month.

4. Dates and Times of all Social Events in and around Herne Bay. 10/- per year entitles you to full programme each week.

Details from . .

"SERVICES"
HERNE BAY 3452

went to our house and looked after 'our' students when they returned from their holidays.

Michelle came to Pembury hospital after school each day and washed and fed me. I was not allowed to do anything for myself. There was a drip in each arm and the bed was raised up at the foot. By this time I also had lung embolisms and so was not allowed to move very much at all. The doctors waited until it was time for my child to be born, the time came and went, no child appeared, and I got progressively weaker.

I learned much later that the Specialist, Mr. Gratsby, had travelled to the Queen Victoria Hospital where Nessa was doing her training, and told her.

"I don't think there is much hope for your mother. We are doing our best but it doesn't seem to be enough. We will try and save her and the baby but."

"You don't know my Mum, she'll be out of there before you can say knife, and so will the baby." Ness said vehemently.

"Well, if she has that much determination I'm sure you will be proved right. We will do everything we can to get the result we all hope for. Would you like me to tell Michelle?

"You can't tell Michelle something like that; she's much to young to be told such things." Ness was seventeen and Michelle just fifteen and a half!

My time to deliver passed by. They did everything they could to help the child come naturally, but neither the baby, or I had the strength for the birth. The anticoagulants used to clear the thrombosis had been withdrawn, and everyone was concerned that the blood would start to clot again. They waited as long as they dared, but had, in the end, to decide on a caesarean delivery. As I was not expected to survive, or the child to live, I made Mr Gratsby promise he would have the child christened as soon as she was born, he gave her the names Claire Elisabeth.

Claire spent the first three weeks of her life on antibiotics, I progressed by leaps and bounds, and when Claire weighed four pounds we were allowed to go home. Nessa came to the hospital and we all went home in triumph in the hospital car. Ness, Michelle, Claire, and me. It was Easter Sunday afternoon, wonderful timing. I was allowed to go home, and to take her home, as long as I did nothing but feed her. I was told

"No housework for you my girl. You can look after your child and yourself nothing more."

The five students were still living in the house, and my friend Connie, who had been running the house for me whilst I was in hospital, had returned to her own home for a rest, and to catch up on things she had neglected while she was at "Essex Lodge." I had then to employ a housekeeper to run the house and feed the students and Michelle. Nessa had gone back to the Queen Vic, and Michelle returned to her old school.

Claire was progressing very well putting on weight fast, and I was getting stronger each day. She was a very beautiful baby, but when I looked at her I knew she was never really totally here.

She gained weight rapidly until, three weeks after we had returned home, the Saturday after my birthday. Claire had not woken up for her 10.00 p.m. feed. Michelle insisted I went up to bed as I had been up since five o clock that morning and was very, very tired.

"Go on, go to bed", Michelle said, "I'll give Claire her feed when she wakes."

I went thankfully, and was asleep almost immediately. I got up on the Sunday morning found Claire was not in her cot, and ran downstairs to see where she was. Michelle had fed Claire the night before, and put her in her carrycot, which was in the dining room. The fire was alight in there, and Michelle thought it would be better to leave her, where it was warm, rather than disturb me by bringing her upstairs.

I made Claire's bottle and waited for her to wake up. She had still not woken at 7.15 am, so I went to wake her up and found that she was stiff and cold. I realised that she was dead. I threw her back in her cot, literally threw her back, and rushed upstairs to Michelle's room, shook her awake and said

"Wake up Michelle, Wake up, Claire's dead."

A terrible thing to do, but that's what I did! She came downstairs with me, took one look at Claire and said,

"Yes, I think she is dead we had better get the doctor." We telephoned for the doctor. Our own doctor was not on duty, and they gave us another number, the number of someone completely unknown to us. He arrived some time later, gave Claire a cursory glance and said, "I'm afraid there is nothing I can do here." and left. He just walked out of the house; he walked out of the house, without asking, "Will you be alright? Is there anything you need?" Nothing, he said nothing to either of us. No explanations were given about what would happen now, what we had to do if anything. Or why, or how, she had died.

Half an hour later an undertaker man came and said he was there to take her away, he put her in what looked like a shoebox. We were not asked if we wanted to see her, or hold her, he just packed her away in his shoebox. I had no idea what I was doing or why, but I insisted that he took everything that had belonged to her, her clothes, her food, bottles, pram and carry- cot, everything. I went all round the house finding everything we had bought for her and made him take it all away with her. He took her in a funny sort of white van and I was not allowed to see her again. When I asked why, they just said it was better that way.

At nine o'clock the policeman came. He questioned and questioned both Michelle and I for hours. After which he said,

"As Claire had not been ill the doctor has had to inform the Coroner of her death. That is why I am here." So this was the reason for his visit. I wished that he had told me that to begin with, I may have understood the reasoning behind his insistent questioning. I had answered his questions calmly. I did not cry. It all seemed to be happening to somebody else, not to me.

By the time he left, Michelle was in a state of shock and crying bitterly. Her boyfriend Keith had arrived. I telephoned the doctor and asked him to come and see Michelle.

"Please come," I pleaded, "She is in a state of shock and needs some help."

He said that Michelle must go to him if she wanted him to see her, as it was supposed to be his day off and he had already made one visit to the house.

So Keith took her in his car and the doctor gave her a sedative of some sort and sent her home to go to bed. When Michelle stopped crying I started. Nessa came home. I do not know who sent for her, I have never known, but she arrived late in the afternoon. It all seemed like an horrific nightmare. The housekeeper had disappeared never to be seen again. The students had to be looked after, the funeral arranged and paid for, all these things were done automatically as if it was all a bad dream. I cried for three months. Three long searing months, then, out of the blue, came a letter from a girl friend I had known way back in time, Denise Wantner. Such a shock, Denise, the girl from Wimbledon, with whom I used to sit in meditation but had not seen for years. The letter informed me that she and a group of friends had held a 'Home Circle' in Denise's house in Wimbledon the week before and at the end of the meeting the guide of the circle had come through to them and said.

"This is a message for one called Sally who is grieving over the loss of Claire Elisabeth. The earth doctors will say that this child died of pneumonia. In fact, it was nothing of the sort. She had only to touch the earth to complete her Karma, to know nothing but love, and to give nothing but love, and she has now gone back from whence she came."

The letter from Denise went on to say,

"I do not know if you will ever get this. I don't know where you are. Your house has been sold and I have been trying to find you for the last two years. This is the address the guide gave me and I can only hope and pray that it is right."

The address was correct in all its details. The name of the house the number of the parade, even the post-code was right. I had last seen Denise when I was still living with my husband. Denise also informed me in her letter that he (my husband) had sold the family home and moved away, all unknown to me.

I had not had any contact with him since the day we all moved out. The guide certainly knew his facts.

This was all quite incredible to me, and I realised that I was selfishly crying for myself, crying for the loss of Claire's physical presence, crying for the fact that I had not been given time to know her, to show her the beauties of the sea, the sun. Crying because she will never wear the pretty dresses we had bought for her. When she was born everyone had been so relieved to know that she was perfect in every way, and as I recovered I had looked forward to helping her grow into a happy well-balanced human being.

I'd previously had five miscarriages and an ectopic pregnancy - (a child that grows in the fallopian tube instead of the womb and which can not possibly survive for more than a few weeks.) My tube had burst one night when the child was twelve weeks; the ambulance was called for to take me to hospital. My husband was informed that I may not survive the journey to the hospital but he chose to remain at home and get some sleep. When the tube burst, I had been screaming with pain for two hours before my husband called the ambulance. Now he needed some sleep, he had to work the following day.

Well that was his excuse for the ambulance men when they asked why he was not coming with me in the ambulance. Those ambulance men came in to see me whenever they were in the vicinity of the hospital; they were the first faces I saw when I came round days later, and of course, seeing them I thought that we had just got to the hospital. They explained that I had been there for over a week and then said

"We were so disgusted with your husband for not coming with you in the ambulance, we determined that the first face you saw when you came back to the land of the living would be a friendly face. Preferably one of us."

When the surgeon performed the operation to remove the remains of the child from the tube, they found another child growing normally in the womb. Two separate conceptions. I was not given this information, and so when I was told to "Be still, and stay in bed, you need your rest." I had not listened. I wanted to get home to my family not lie here. The child in the womb miscarried two weeks later. If I had been told of the second child's existence, I would not have moved a muscle.

I remembered all of these things in the weeks following Claire's death and was feeling very sorry for myself. The knowledge that Claire was probably my last chance to have another child was playing on my selfish mind. I was pulled up short by the letter from Denise and made to see how very selfish I was being. Had I not had irrefutable proof that Spirit is working for and with me if only I will let them? How else would I have had the letter from Denise? I had two beautiful daughters and I should be grateful for that instead of bemoaning my lot.

Michelle was now attending her old school again and studying for her 'O' Levels. I have learned since that she had to put up with a tremendous amount of 'name calling' and nastiness when she returned to her school. They thought that as she had been absent from school for three months and we had come home with a baby, that the baby was hers.

Poor Michelle, she said not a word to me about it at the time. She must have suffered a great deal, but kept her pain from me thinking I had enough to cope with.

After Claire died I decided 1 must work, work, work, and not give myself time to think about anything. The students had left for the summer holidays, so I did bed and breakfasts for summer visitors in the house, and ran an ice cream parlour and snack bar for the town's entertainment's department. These premises were immediately opposite the house at the head of the pier, and it was all wonderfully convenient for me. I was up at 5.30 a.m., did the breakfasts for the guests with Michelle's help as she was on vacation. At 7.30 I went across the road to the shop, made the ice cream and got the place ready for the girl assistants who mostly arrived at 9.00 a.m. Then it was back to the house to wash up the breakfast dishes, make the beds, and clean the rooms ready for the next guests. Then over again to the ice cream parlour. People came from miles around for my ice cream. I made it there in the shop, and even though I say it myself it was the best ice cream I have ever tasted. If the weather was good, tables and chairs were put out on the green in front of the shop and we served coffees, teas and cold drinks. I closed the ice cream parlour at 7.00 p.m. and that was when I opened the snack bar.

In this snack bar, next to the 'parlour,' I had a hot dog stand, a doughnut maker, and a small domestic chip fryer. I sold chicken and chips, sausage and chips, hot dogs and doughnuts. Sometimes the queue stretched from the counter to the road, a distance of about fifty yards. They all had a very long wait as the chip fryer only held two portions of chips at a time, but they all insisted it was worth the wait. My customers and I would laugh and joke together and I was called many names, some more complimentary than others were. They all preferred my chips to those from the chippy because,

"Your chips are crisper, and they don't stick to the paper."

I stayed in the snack bar until there was not another soul on the seafront. Everywhere was shut up and empty. Sometimes it was 3.00 a m, then, putting up the heavy wooden shutters which never seemed to want to do what I wanted them to, and making sure all was secure, I closed up. After this I staggered across the road to the house, and fell into a bath, washed the smell of doughnuts from my hair and went to bed, hair still dripping wet, to get up at 5 30 and start again. I did this seven days a week.

All this a few weeks after being told by hospital staff,

"You must do nothing but feed your child, no work of any kind for you my girl for a long time."

The body is an amazing thing - or is it the mind? What say you?

Many years later, Nessa and I were lying in my bed in my first floor flat in London. She was staying with me for a few days - my flat is only a few yards from the road and the front of the house is often very noisy at night. We had put the big bed in my bedroom in the middle of the flat and we shared that. After spending a long time chattering about this and that, we had a game or two of 'I spy' then decided it was time to put out the light and go to sleep. For some unknown reason I had left the bedroom door open, something I had never done before and have not done since. As we lay quietly happy in the dark, I thought about Claire Elisabeth, and I said to Nessa, "I wonder what would have happened to US if Claire had lived. Our lives would have been totally different, wouldn't they?"

I had never posed that question to myself or to anyone else. I HAD often wondered what Claire would have been like, and what would she be doing now, but never, "What would have happened to us?"

"Yes Mum," said Ness "I suppose they would."

I then said, "I have never forgiven myself for not giving Claire her last feed."

At that moment the landing outside the bedroom door was flooded with a white light, the whitest light I had ever seen. Not a bright light, a WHITE light. The light hung there for two seconds, and it was gone. Back again for a second or two, and then funereal blackness, the light was gone.

The light did not come into the bedroom or the sitting room at the front of the flat; it just flooded the landing. The whiteness was so brilliant yet not at all uncomfortable to look at. We stared at it Ness and I, without it hurting our eyes.

"What was that? What's going on?" Nessa said as she leapt out of bed.

I have never seen her move so fast. She rushed into the sitting room to see if there was a car in the street which might have caused the light but nothing stirred; there were no cars, no people, the street was deserted.

We tried hard to work out what could have made a light appear on my first floor landing. If it had come in through the window of the sitting room it would also have bathed that room in its glow, but the room had remained unlit, just as the bedroom we were in had stayed dark.

So what was the answer? We tried very hard to find a plausible one but could not. It would be so wonderful to think that Claire had been with us, listening to our conversations and had come bringing the light with her to say,

"Its all right Mum, I do know how you feel. There really isn't any need for you to concern yourself. It was my time to die that night, and whatever you did or didn't do, it would have made not the slightest difference."

But in the absence of any tangible proof I can only say "That's a lovely thought and wouldn't it be super if it were so?"

FIRST EXPERIENCE OF SEEING PEOPLE 'EN MASSE'

My Aunt Nell had moved out to Hatch End in Middlesex soon after the war and we stayed in contact with each other. Both she and my cousins, her sons, had shown great interest in what was happening to me in a psychic way. In the late sixties she asked me to go to Hatch End as there were a number of people known to her who were in need of healing and/or help in a psychic way.

I went to meet her at the address she had given me over the telephone, and to my astonishment found it to be a pub! I walked in and was astounded to see that my Mother was sitting tucked up in the corner of the room. So not only were my Aunt Nell and a good number of people I did not know waiting expectantly, but my Mother was there too! Mother rarely visited anyone, as she did not have a car, and found public transport difficult to cope with. Mother and Aunt sat and watched while I saw one person after another, and when the last one had been seen and gone, my cousin Stan took us all back to my Aunt's house where Mother was staying for the night.

When we arrived at the house my Mother looked at me searchingly and said,

"You have given so much to so many people tonight. Now what have you to say to me?"

I took her in my arms, longing to give her some comfort and prayed for the right words to say, but there was no response to my prayers. There was nothing I could say, or do to comfort her; it was as though I were holding a completely empty shell. It was one of the worst moments of my life.

Mother stayed with Aunt Nell that night, and I went home with Stan who lived a couple of houses along the street.

I saw Mother for a short while before I returned home the next morning, and although I knew she was in need of help and comfort, there was still nothing of substance that I could say to her. I felt dreadful but there was nothing I could do. I suppose I could have lied and told her, "Your dear little Mum is here for you." but she would have known I was just trying to cheer her up, and I would know that I had cheated her.

Years later, I consulted an astrologer friend Howard Sasporta, and mentioned how distraught I had been at that time. He told me that many years before, my Mother had had to allow her Spirit to 'leave' as it had nothing to learn from the things that were happening to her at that time in her life. It had meant either, letting her Spirit go, or going mad. Mother chose to allow her Spirit to go, they had already been through these travails together in previous lives, and her Spirit had no need to travel that road again.

She chose to live out her life where she was, in spite of all the pain and suffering this was to cause her, hoping that at some time before her death she would once more regain her Spirit. This explained the feeling that I was holding an empty shell when I took her in my arms. She had a great many heartaches in her life mainly caused by those dearest to her.

We had very little communication at any time during her stay on earth, I remember the one and only time she put her arm round me, it was the first day of my first period. She met me at the gate put her arm round me and said,

"You mustn't get your feet wet at a time like this."

As my feet were already saturated I was terrified. What would happen to me now, would I catch a fever and die? But the moment was gone and I was given no more information. Mother was back in her shell.

Even though I tried very hard over the last few years of her life to put things right between us, it was to no avail. I was not told of her final illness until it was too late for there to be any chance of my talking with her. She was being given massive doses of morphine by the time I got to the hospital and although I stayed with her until she died, she did not, could not, speak with me.

I know there is no point in spending time on recriminations or regrets, but I would have liked to have been able to talk with her. To ask her what she would have liked to do with her life if things had been different. What were her hopes and dreams? Did she ever have any? Or did she, like me, just go along with whatever came her way?

It would have been so good to tell her how I wished that we could have had the sort of relationship that I now saw other mothers and daughters having. I also wanted to tell her how I feared that my daughters and I would end up the same way, not having any communication, if we, Mother and I, could not - put it right; Selfish me.

But it is done and can not be undone, as Omar Khayyam wrote,

'The moving finger writes; and having writ, moves on: nor all thy Piety nor wit shall lure it back to cancel half a line, Nor all they tears wash out a word of it.'

THE EFFECTS OF PREVIOUS LIVES.

I was told by a well-known clairvoyant, Cyril Macklin, that in a previous life I had been in a position of great power, a ruling position, and had misused that power. I had to learn to use power correctly in this life. That was why I had chosen to come back, to redress the balance so to speak.

I suppose I started to see people professionally to try to do just that, to 'put it right,' to use power correctly. Sometimes when the ego bit of me comes up I get quite cross about the fact that I still have nothing. I work very hard and always succeed with whatever I do, then let it all go. I think I need a fresh challenge; I guess I am still frightened of the responsibilities and power that success brings.

Although I have accepted that it is all right to charge my clients for doing Readings I still do not charge for healing. I have always said that healing should not be charged for.

I decided recently that as healing was taking up a great deal of my time, I would put out a box for free-will offerings, to help with my rent and overheads. A sensible move I thought, but then what did I do? - I told the ones that come regularly and to whom 1 give most of my time

"Don't worry, it's not there for you. Of course, YOU don't need to give anything!"

MATCHES AND ROSES

I was staying with Alan, a friend of mine, and he wanted to put up some shelves in our room and needed to find some rawlplugs. I suggested that he use matches to plug the holes for the screws. I had always used them and found them quite adequate.

He, being a Virgo, and a perfectionist, would not hear of it, and he spent ages searching through the tool bags for rawlplugs. He then went out to the shed to see if he could find some out there.

When he came back I was standing in the doorway between our room and the kitchen, and he came in through the kitchen door from the garden. The kitchen stretched between us.

I asked "Any luck?"

"No!" He fumed.

At that moment, two matches floated gently down from the ceiling and landed on the floor between us. The matches seemed to be falling in slow motion and we both stood and stared in utter amazement. Neither of us used matches and there were certainly none in the flat, so where had these matches come from? We couldn't find a rational explanation, where had they come from? We were very puzzled by their sudden appearance for weeks afterwards; after all there really were no matches in the flat. But Alan did use matches, which he went out to buy, to put up those shelves, muttering something very uncomplimentary about 'witches' under his breath!

Alan and I shared a house, which backed onto Wandsworth Common with a number of other people, graphic designers and artists. A gate at the end of the garden led directly onto a path across the common. During the weeks I stayed with Alan, we both noticed a strong smell of roses at various times, in the kitchen and the room that we shared. The scent was most powerful, and all of us who shared the house searched very hard to find its source with no success. There were no roses in bloom in the garden, it being the wintertime; and neither of us used any lotion or perfumes, which smelt remotely like roses. It was a complete mystery, until the day when I decided to walk across the Common to the local shops.

I had bought the things I needed from the grocer and found myself wandering into the chemist. One of the assistants came forward and asked, "Can I help you?"

"Oh, no, no thank you I don't know what I am doing in here, there must be some reason but I really don't know what it is."

"Well," he replied, "Have a look round, you may see something you want."

So saying, he resumed the conversation with his colleagues that I had interrupted when I walked in. I wandered round the shop and could not see anything that I wished to buy, so I went to find the man who had spoken so kindly to me when I entered the shop, to thank him for his courtesy.

As I approached the little knot of men who were talking animatedly, I heard the name 'George Wilmott.'

My heart leapt and I must have looked quite dreadful because one of the men offered me a chair saying

"Here, steady on! You'd better sit down here for while. Would you like some water? Yes, get her some water Jack, she looks as though she's seen a ghost." Little did he know how close to the truth his words were. Jack bought me a glass of water and after I had recovered I asked the man,

"Did I hear you correctly, were you talking about someone called George Willmot?"

"Yes, that's right, we were. Why, did you know him?"

"Is the George Wilmott you are talking about a doctor who stopped practising medicine a number of years ago and lives in Battersea?"

"Well, yes, he was a doctor, but he has been living rough for some months, he was found dead a few weeks ago in thick hedges over the other side of the Common."

"Oh, I see," I took a deep breath and tried to allow what I had just heard sink in. "Now I know why I had to come into your shop. It wasn't to buy anything; it was to hear that news about George Wilmott. He was a dear friend of mine many years ago."

As I spoke, the shop was filled with the scent of roses.

I ran back across the Common to tell Alan what I had learned. I had known George the doctor when I lived near Clapham Junction and was pregnant with my second child. He had shown me great kindness and, despite the fact that he had no income and survived on handouts, he brought me food when I had none.

I was living in one room with my first child Nessa, and her father we had very little money as he refused to do any work. I was pregnant with our second child. Quite often during that time I was startled by an object landing on the bed. When I investigated I would, more often than not, find it was a parcel of food, some times even an unwrapped fish he had managed to obtain, I never queried where these things came from, I thought it best if I remained ignorant! They were thrown in through the ever-open window by the Dr. Willmot. The window was permanently open, because it could not be closed; the sash cords had broken inside the frame and were jammed. Dr Wilmott would climb in the window after the food, and we then shared whatever he had bought after I had cooked it on my Primus stove.

He always said he would rather bring me roses and promised that 'one day' he would fill my room with them. He certainly did just that, although not in the way I had expected at the time. When he did manage to do it, almost twenty years later, I had forgotten all about that promise, and about him. I had only seen him once in the intervening years, when I was living in Sevenoaks and had been visiting someone in Clapham. We had met quite by chance in the street. He was lodging in a hostel nearby and seemed content, in spite of the fact that he had tipped a kettle of boiling water over his foot a few days previously.

We talked for a while and I told him of my second marriage; about the children, and how they were both doing well. Nessa at this time was at Brampton Down School in Folkestone, and Michelle in Monaco at the Diaghilev School of Russian Classical Ballet - and after an hour or so we went our separate ways.

That was the last I had heard of him until I walked into the chemist shop on Wandsworth Common, with no idea at all why, or what I was doing in there.

A few months after this, I had moved into a flat in Bayswater, and Alan brought an American friend of his to see me. We were sitting in my flat in Chepstow Place having a cup of tea, and his friend was talking about something or other that I knew to be untrue.

I found myself saying, "That's not true, that's not true! Give me your hand."

As I looked at his hand, I told him he had had a row with his girlfriend, (who was named) and they that would make it up when he returned to America. The relationship would not last and he would meet someone else who would be right for him and bring him great happiness.

Many other things were spoken of which astounded him, as he was sure that no one else could possibly have known about any of those things.

He was also told "You have been doing a lot of writing, using a giant pencil and then scrubbing some of it out. You must not do this; you must leave it as it comes. Spirit is guiding you to write the truth in a way that everyone will understand. IT MUST NOT BE CHANGED, please leave it as it is when you first write it."

When we were talking about it later, he asked me, "Why did you use the words 'giant pencil'?"

I said, "I don't know, I have no idea why those words were used. I never know what is going to be said, I just hear it as it is being said, and very seldom remember it unless it is important for me to know something about that person. If that person poses a threat to me in some way I will remember, otherwise I don't recall any of the conversation."

He gave me a strange look and then told me that he HAD been

writing, using a pencil bought for him by the pupils of his class as an end-of-term present. And he had scrubbed a lot of it out.

This pencil he had been using was eighteen inches long and an inch thick. Yes, indeed, it was a giant pencil!

He was a teacher in America and had been surprised to find that he had the urge to write things he had not even thought about before. The writing had flowed but he had felt he should change it, as he could not understand why it was so easy! He had been brought up to believe that anything that comes easily must be wrong - we must work very hard if it is to be any good.

Three months after 'the American' had returned home, Alan received a letter saying that he had indeed made it up with his girlfriend, but the relationship had not lasted and he had now met someone else, with whom he was very happy.

He also enclosed some photographs that he had taken when he was on his visit to England and while he was staying in Alan's flat.

When they were being taken, I had told him, there would be phenomena of some kind on one of these photographs when they were developed.

Sure enough, one of them had what looked like a large white flame running right across the picture. It was one he had taken of me standing by the rose bushes at the end of the garden! George Willmot, paying a visit?

Alan is a graphic designer and I continued to take his work to publishers after I had moved into the flat in Bayswater. Although I knew nothing about artwork or the terms used by art directors, I very seldom went out without bringing a commission for some artwork back for him to do.

He is still working with the contacts I made for him during that time.

FAMILY LINKS THROUGH TELEPATHY?

It was a very warm evening, as I walked home after having spent the afternoon at Young and Rubicans for Alan, I was surprised to see some of my friends sitting outside our local pub 'The Chepstow'. They invited me to join them, but I declined saying,

"No thanks, much too early for me. It's only 7 o'clock."

"Oh, come on, have a half of bitter, it will do you good, cool you down a bit."

So, I agreed. We usually met in the pub at about ten o'clock in the evening. We very seldom went in much before that time. There were a group of about eighteen of us who met up fairly regularly; our ages ranged from eighteen to eighty, and we sat and chatted or had a game of darts, depending on how energetic we were feeling! And then we quite often tumbled down to my flat to talk and eat or dance the night away.

I asked, "What are you doing here at this early hour?"

They had no idea; it had just seemed a good thing to do, as it was such a warm evening.

Soon after I had been given my drink, Lindy, a very good friend, arrived with her boyfriend John. They were supposed to be going on a trip down the river, because it was Lindy's birthday; but the person who had promised to take them had not turned up and John could not think of anywhere else to take her, so he had brought her to the pub! I was very cross with him and wanted to do something to help make Lindy feel better and enjoy her birthday.

All of our friends turned up, one after the other, none knowing why they had decided to come so early, and I whispered to all of them as they came in,

"It's Lindy's birthday, say Happy Birthday to Lindy."

They rummaged in their bags and pockets and each of them found something they could give her for her birthday, or they bought her a drink. By eight-thirty there was a swinging party going on in the pub. Every one was enjoying them selves, but I felt vaguely uneasy and I knew that I had to go down to my flat, which was next door to the pub. Why, I did not know. I just knew I had to go. I kept saying to myself,

"This is silly. What am I doing? There is a super party going on here. Why don't I stay? Why do I have to go to my flat?"

I tried to convince myself that I did not have to go: but down I went, and then found myself getting undressed and getting into bed, still thinking,

"This is ridiculous! I am not tired. Why do I need to go to bed? It's still only half past eight for goodness sake."

I woke up with a start. It was dark. What had woken me? I switched on the lights looked at the clock and saw that it was ten minutes to eleven. What? Christopher Columbus! I had been asleep for over two hours. I sat up, dazed and still sleepy, and was brought back to reality with a jolt when I remembered... my dream.

In my dream I was watching my daughter Nessa, walking alone along the pavement of a very busy main road looking distressed, and absolutely lost.

I was saying to her "Look up Nessa, look up!"

I was sure that she could hear me because she turned round anxiously trying to find out where the voice was coming from. I continued saying,

"Look up Nessa, look up!"

After a while she looked up. Her face brightened and she hurried away.

At midnight the telephone rang. It was Nessa.

"How are you?" I asked. "Why are you ringing me at this time of night, can't you sleep?"

"I've had a bit of an accident, but I'm fine now." she replied.

"What do you mean, I've had a bit of an accident, but I'm fine now? What has happened?"

"I was riding my motorbike."

"Motorbike," I broke in, "what motorbike? I didn't know you had a motorbike!"

"Yes, I have, I do have one now. I was riding it around the garden that's full of potholes. I hit the edge of one, fell off my bike and knocked myself out. The people in the house called an ambulance to take me to hospital, but it took ages to come! When I eventually got to the hospital they examined me, and said I hadn't done any serious damage and that I could go home." She went on, "I know that I walked out of the hospital gates, but then I don't remember anything else until I became aware that I was walking down a main street in a strange place. I kept walking, not knowing where I was, until I found myself on East Ham High Street."

"How did you find out where you were?" I asked.

"I didn't. I didn't know where I was. I was totally lost until, I don't know how to explain this it was so strange - but I knew that I must look up. I looked up and saw the name 'East Ham High Street,' then I knew where I was and I came home."

"What time did you get home?" I asked.

"Ten minutes to eleven. Why mum, is it important?"

Ten minutes to eleven was the time I had woken from my strange dream! I knew then why I had gone to my bed so early. Spirit needed me to be asleep to take MY 'Spirit' to Ness, and help her to get home.

But, Nessa had said she had come off her bike at twenty to nine. So it wasn't because she had mentally called me as she fell that I had gone down to my flat at eight-thirty. If I had gone down at eight-forty or eight forty-five, it could be said to be telepathy or something of this sort. But not ten minutes before it happened. So what was it?

This link between members of a family is well attested to by many people and, seems to go beyond the 'simple telepathy' that most people like to label it.

Another example of the strength of this link between my elder daughter and myself occurred at about eleven o'clock on the evening of my birthday in 1970, when I was again very concerned about her. I was still living in Herne Bay at the time and had not heard from her. Even if she did not contact me for the rest of the year, she always sent a card or telephoned me on my birthday.

I was talking to Tony, an artist friend who was living in the house, and I said to him,

"I don't know why she hasn't written and I am very worried. I know she can't call me here with the telephone not working but she usually finds some way of contacting me."

He said "Well, why don't you sit quietly and ask for some guidance, or at least to be shown what's happening to her?"

"I don't want to intrude on her privacy."

"You wouldn't be concerned about her if she were not trying to contact you in some way, would you?" he said.

I had to agree he was right. So we sat quietly and I asked, - if it was morally and spiritually right for me to know - to be shown where she was, and what was happening in her life to make me so concerned about her. After sitting quietly for some time I 'saw' her, in a room where everything seemed to be red. She was sitting on what looked like a black box, with a policeman standing over her, his arm around her shoulders. I saw her crying bitterly, something she very rarely does. The scene changed and I was shown a bridge over a river. The sides of the bridge were of an open pattern and I could see through them.

Some men were pulling a large object, which looked like a box covered in black polythene, out of the river. I thought 'Oh my goodness! Nessa and her girlfriend have had a row and the girl has thrown herself in the river. That's what it is, and the men have had to pull her out! That would explain why Ness is crying, and what the policeman is doing there.'

The scene changed and I was then shown a very wide street, with the brightest of orange lights casting an eerie glow over everything. I had never seen bright orange lights on any street before, and wondered where they were. I knew it was a main road and very busy, but there was no way of knowing why it was being shown to me. That it was important there was no doubt but nothing more. I told Tony what I had seen, leaving nothing out and adding nothing. He said,

"Well, what do you think it all means?"

I, of course, was trying to put my own interpretation on it, putting two and two together and making fifteen. I was very concerned to see her crying because, as I have said, it is not something she does easily.

And the policeman - what was he doing there? I willed her to contact me somehow. My telephone was not working so I knew she could not phone me at home. But I willed her,

"Please Nessa, contact me somehow. Please let me know what is happening and where you are - please God make her contact me."

About half an hour later someone came banging frantically on the door, it was Neil, the younger son of the couple who owned the hotel two or three doors along. He said,

"Please come, you are wanted on the telephone."

With my heart pounding I ran along the road to the hotel. It was with great relief that I heard Nessa's voice saying

"Happy birthday Mum."

"Thank goodness for that, are you all right?" I asked.

"Yes, Mum, I am all right, why do you ask?"

"Why have you been crying, and what was the policeman doing with his arm around you?"

"A car hit me earlier this evening when I went across the road to get some change to telephone you. I'm not hurt.

I was badly shaken, but I'm not hurt."

"Were you on a wide road and were there bright orange lights?" I asked.

"Yes, it was Ilford High Road. Why are you asking? How did you know there are orange lights there, they've only just changed them?"

I asked her, "Darling, is your room red, and what was the black box you were sitting on?"

"Oh yes, all the walls of the room now have red wallpaper. It's all been redecorated and I was sitting on a new telephone seat we have bought which is black."

"Well -what has a river and something black and shiny got to do with it?" I asked, thinking of the scene I had witnessed where the men were

81

pulling something from the river.

"The car that hit me was black, and apparently had just been through a ford in the river, just outside Ilford, and had to be pulled out. The water had got into the brakes, which is why he couldn't stop when he saw me. The policeman ran and picked me up, took me indoors and stayed to comfort me."

"But you are all right?"

"Yes, Mum, I am fine. I just wanted to wish you a happy birthday. I was going to phone you earlier but obviously, with all this bother, I couldn't."

I said "It's all right, it's fine as long as you are all right. That is all that matters."

She has told me since that she and her girlfriend had been evicted from their flat and they were squatting in a Chinese restaurant owned by friends of theirs, this accounted for the red wallpaper and black telephone seat! She did not tell me at the time because she knew I would be concerned, and would want to go to her and help.

Now I know whenever I find myself going to bed when I am not tired, or refuse to see a client, it is for a very good reason.

Sometimes I even find myself saying,

"I can't see you today I'm sorry." to a client who has booked an appointment with me.

The people, who work with, or for me, find this latter thing, very difficult to cope with. But, I know it is because there has been an accident or something is happening somewhere, and 'the management' or someone out there, needs a helping hand.

Sometimes it is because my client should be somewhere else, there is some one waiting for them, unknown to them but necessary in their life at this time. I have learned not to question these feelings.

LONDON 1971 HEALING

During the 70's I occasionally visited the Spiritualist Association of Great Britain at 33 Belgrave Square to listen to the lectures. I had arranged to meet some friends there one night in 1971 to listen to Bertha Harris talking about the Aura. David, one of the other mediums came along whilst the people I was with were going in.

I had been very concerned for David for a few months; he was working far too hard and long, and was being taken over by his little girl Spirit helper. I knew, if he didn't take some time off, AND stop working completely during that time off, he would almost certainly be very sick. If he kept working in the way he was doing he would need months to recover, instead of the weeks he needed now.

I told him how I felt and stood outside the lecture hall chattering with him for a while.

When I eventually walked into the room there was only one seat left, right at the front, so I had to take that. I was amazed but not surprised to find that I was seated next to a man my daughter Michelle and I had met there the previous Sunday. We were sitting in the cafe, which was in the basement of the S.A.G.B, and he had asked if he could join us at our table. He told us his name was Boris and he was here from Sweden investigating Spiritualism on a scientific level making tapes of readings and interviews and analysing them.

Mrs. Harris gave her talk, and then said she would demonstrate how sickness could be diagnosed through the Aura. After talking with a number of people she indicated Boris, the man sitting next to me, and told him he would be cured by healing as he had something wrong with his back.

"No, I don't think so, not with healing or anything else. I have been to Specialists all over the world and there is nothing that can be done by anyone!" He answered her vigorously.

"You will be cured by healing, and there is the one who is going to do it." she said, pointing directly at me. I cringed with embarrassment as everyone in the room craned forward to look at me. She asked me

"Are you two together?"

"No," I said, "Why do you ask that?"

"Because your Aura shook when I came to him."

I had known there was something wrong with his back and had been sitting with my hand behind him, along the top of the seats, asking for healing to take place, while I was listening to the lecture. The reason my Aura shook was because I was scared stiff she was going to talk about my life and health! And then to be told in public "You will heal this man." was too much for me. Mrs. Harris told me of some trouble I had had with my legs. This she could see in my aura.

The information was accurate, so I was afraid she was accurate about this man as well! - And that he would expect me to work miracles.

I felt I was not ready to accept that sort of responsibility and tried to duck out of it by ignoring him, but he found me after the meeting and asked me for my name and address. I did not want to give it to him, as I did not think I could live up to Mrs. Harris's recommendations. I gave him my telephone number and thought 'If he calls I can always say I am busy.'

What a dreadful thing to plan to do, but that is what I did and hoped that he would not ring. He did ring, every day - but it was Friday morning before I made arrangements to see him. I said he could come to tea at 4 o'clock on Friday afternoon. I was still unwilling to accept the responsibility for someone else's health! I knew he had to return to Sweden on the Saturday, so I had stalled and put him off as long as I could.

He arrived at exactly 4.00 p.m., and, after I had taken his coat and hat, - he always wore a black beret, - and given him some tea, he told me that he had a sitting at the College of Psychic Studies that morning. It had been a trance sitting which he had taped and he now played the tape for me to hear.

At this trance sitting, the guide told him that he had been to the college the year before, and at that time he had been told that he would come back this year. He, at that time, had denied this vehemently, and had said, "No, I will not, I will not come to this country again."

"But there he was - so they had been right, hadn't they?" The guide went on to say, "At that time, you were told you will meet someone when you came back this time, and that this person was going to be very important to you." Boris had interjected here and said

"That's right, but it hasn't happened. If it is going to happen it had better hurry up because I am going back to Sweden tomorrow."

He was then told, "You have already met her. You are going to tea with her at four o'clock this afternoon."

The tape ended abruptly. He was looking at me expectantly. I thought 'this is dreadful what do I do now?' I knew he was expecting some healing and I was not at all sure of how to go about it with Boris. I had the feeling that he was not just looking for healing and I was a bit uneasy. I may have done him an injustice, but, "better safe than sorry", as my Grandma would say. After procrastinating as long as I could I thought, I may as well get it over and done with, and just be very careful where and how I put my hands.

I never think anything is going to happen with healing or readings and when it does, no one is more surprised than me. However, Boris was given some healing, and he seemed to benefit from it.

As he had nowhere to stay in London, he stayed the night sleeping on my sofa. (I was grateful for the intuitive warning) He had some more healing the next morning and returned to Sweden mid-day Saturday. We arranged to sit quietly at eleven o'clock each evening in prayer, asking for healing for him, he in Sweden, me in London. He telephoned often and wrote each week, saying that he was a little better every day, his back was getting stronger and he was free of pain for longer periods.

Then, one evening three months later, he telephoned to say that he was in hospital.

I was shattered. Why? What was he doing there? They had diagnosed cancer in his throat. He had had many investigations and examinations and these proved beyond doubt that he had a cancerous growth and they were going to operate the next day.

"Please ask for some healing. Please do something." He begged. I promised I would try.

I replaced the receiver and made myself comfortable, as I knew I was in for a long session. I said all the prayers I could remember asking for the healing power to be directed to his throat.

I sat through the next few days and nights concentrating on him, visualising him fit and well on the screen in my mind. His throat clear and healthy, blood pure, and body whole.

I continued to do this until I 'Knew' there was no longer any necessity to ask for him.

A week or so later, the telephone rang and there, on the other end of a crackling line was Boris, sounding strong and healthy.

"Where are you?" I asked, "You sound fine."

"I am, I'm at home!"

"But, what are you doing at home? I thought you were at deaths door in hospital."

"Yes, I was, but, they took me to the operating theatre, opened me up and found nothing, no sign of cancer.

No tumour, no cancer, nothing life threatening. So they sent me home, unable to believe that what had been there, and proved to be there, one day, had gone the next. I feel so good, and I wanted to thank you for your thoughts and prayers, they obviously worked!"

We are still in contact with one another and his back is fit and strong. He is now a qualified Psychotherapist, using his newly found health to help others.

HELPING TO CREATE A YOUNG MILLIONAIRE

Some time during my stay in Chepstow Place the washing machine had broken down and I went to see if Morris, the manager of 'The Chepstow,' knew of an odd job man who could fix it. He did not. While we stood speculating about the situation Morris pulled me a half of bitter, which I sat down to drink, and one of two young men seated at the bar opened up a conversation. He introduced himself as Melvyn and said he would come and have a look at the washing machine to see if he could do anything to put it right.

We finished our drinks and went into the house. He spent an hour or so working on the machine. When he had finished, the machine was working perfectly.

I offered him a cup of tea and while we were sitting talking, I 'saw' in my mind, a large elegant house, and asked him,

"Are you thinking of moving?"

"No." he answered, "Why"?

"Then do you live in a house that looks like this?"

I said, and I did a drawing of the house I had seen in my mind.

"No, no I live in a flat in Earls Court, but I'm thinking of buying a house which looks just like that."

"Is it number?" (I cannot actually remember what number it was now).

"Yes it is. How did you know that?" he said.

"Then buy it, it will be a very good thing to do and make you a very rich man."

He did, - and it was a very good investment. That was the start of his property speculation. Whenever Melvyn was looking at anything with a view to buying it over the next two years, he would come and see me not mentioning any thing about the proposed purchase.

If, during the course of our conversation, I SAW the place he was interested in, he would buy it, if not, he left it alone.

He came at other times as well, so there was never a time anyone could say,

"Oh well, if he only came to see you when he was thinking of buying something, of course you would get it right."

He often brought people in need of healing or just for a chat and a 'cuppa'. The houses he bought all proved to be very profitable for him.

I do not know if the ones I had not seen would have been so successful, there is no way of telling. Perhaps they would have been, or maybe he could have lost a great deal of money. As it was, he became a millionaire at the age of twenty-three, through property speculation.

The house in which I had my flat next to 'The Chepstow' was put on the market with vacant possession. Melvyn offered more for it than was being asked because he wanted to be sure he would get it, and so ensure that I was able to keep my flat. The owner, 'J' who was young and very beautiful, could not understand why a young man would want to pay more than was being asked, just so that I, a 'much older woman,' would be able to stay in my flat. She refused to sell the house to him.

It had been promised to friends of hers at the original price, which was way below the true market value. 'J', the owner, of the house was not in need of money. These friends bought the house, but never lived in it. One of the couple who bought it died before they had a chance of moving in. It was resold later to a religious group. So I lost my beautiful flat.

Melvyn also offered to give me £3,000 a year, a lot of money then.

"What for?" I asked.

"For what you have been doing for nothing up to now, being my mentor and helping me to help other people." he replied.

"Oh, but no, I couldn't. If I accepted money it wouldn't work, nothing would come. I'm sure nothing would happen."

"How do you know? You have helped to make me a very wealthy man, so money can't be all that bad."

"I know, but that's for you, not for me."

So saying I refused his generous offer. Stupid girl. I still had this very silly attitude that psychic gifts are given freely to be given freely, and must not be charged for.

As the house had been sold with vacant possession, I had to move. I rented a house out at Hampton Hill and we lost touch, or so I thought!

It was some years later when I was back in Notting Hill Gate that I heard of a new restaurant opening in Chelsea and it occurred to me to go and have a look at it - something I had never done before, and have not done since.

When I arrived the place was buzzing, with hundreds of people milling around on the ground floor and as far as I could tell, many more in the basement.

Handing the man on the door my coat and gloves, I was offered a glass of champagne which I was just about to take when a great commotion started round me. People were getting pretty cross because someone was pushing his way through, and climbing over, them from the back of the crowded ground floor room.

It was Melvyn, the young man from Chepstow Place. He had seen me come in and wanted to be one of the first to greet me. Melvyn informed me that he had bought and refurbished the restaurant. "I also have a stud farm at Ascot."

I was introduced to everyone there as his 'mentor,' and they were all informed in no uncertain manner, that if it had not been for me needing someone to repair a washing machine, he would still be a very poor boy living in a bed-sit in Earls Court. I had a most enjoyable evening, and left promising to keep in touch this time!

STREET CONTACT. RUNNING THE HOSTEL.

A few years later, I was running a hostel for mothers and babies in North London and on my night off I decided to go over to 'The Chepstow' to see my old friends. By ten o'clock I FELT that something was wrong at the hostel.

I telephoned my flat where someone was supposed to be answering my telephones and there was no answer. I then rang the public telephone in the hall of the house.

There were ten girls staying in the hostel, but no one answered. I tried first one phone then the other for fifteen minutes.

Eventually I said to Graham, one of my friends in the pub

"I must go. I think there is something wrong at the hostel. No one is answering any of the telephones."

He was used to my 'knowings' as he called them, and he said

"OK, I'll walk with you to Notting Hill Gate and we'll find a taxi to take you back to Aubert Park."

We walked to Notting Hill Gate and waited for a taxi to come along. As we were standing there a girl came along the street, crying her heart out. When she reached where we were standing I knew I had to speak to her. So I approached her and said,

"Come on now, what is it? You mustn't cry like this."

She fell into my arms, and we stood thus until her sobs had subsided. After a few minutes she said,

"I'm OK now, I must go home."

"Will you be all right?" I asked.

"Yes, yes I'm fine.," she said, wiping away the tears which were still flowing.

"Where do you have to go?"

"Earls Court." she said.

"OK let's go down and see if there is a train for you. Do you have enough money?"

"Yes, Yes thank you, I have enough."

We went down to the tube station at Notting Hill Gate and I made sure there was a train going her way.

I then asked her, "Do you want to talk to someone about it? Would you like to tell me why you were crying?"

"No, it is just something to do with me and my boyfriend. I'll be all right now. Just to know there is someone in London who cares enough to do something when they see another human being crying is enough. Good night, and thank you very much." and off she ran to catch her train, turning to wave before disappearing down the escalator.

I said to Graham, "Right, come on. Let's get back to 'The Chepstow'. I obviously don't need to go to the hostel. The only reason I was made to think about the place was because they, 'The Management' knew that if I thought something was wrong there, I would want to return immediately or take action to find out what it was."

Graham said "I think I can get my head round that, but why 'make' you go all the way to the 'Gate'?"

"Someone who cared just had to be here at the corner of Notting Hill Gate, for when the girl came along to help her for a while until she had got over the worst of it." I told him.

He laughed and said, "Of course, how simple you make it all sound, I suppose it is simple to you!"

We got back to the pub just as they were calling 'last orders', and I managed to get a drink before I left to return to North London. I never did find out why it was that no one had answered the telephones at the hostel that night. It seems that this was another case of 'The Management' getting their own way, - or was it just 'coincidence'?

FOOTBALL FANS ON THE RAMPAGE.

Sitting by the window of my ground floor flat in the hostel, I was keeping an eye on the entrance of the drive to make sure no one blocked it by parking across it.

My friend Gordon was due to arrive to take me to lunch, and then come back with me to do some maintenance work on the back wall.

The hostel was immediately opposite the Arsenal football Ground. It was one fifteen on a Saturday afternoon, and I had completely forgotten when I arranged for Gordon to come, that there was a football match that afternoon between the Arsenal club and Manchester United. The whole area was already crammed with cars and coaches.

A large car pulled up and stopped in the only space available right across the entrance to the hostel! The driver climbed out, looked about him, decided that this was a good place to park and proceeded to lock the car door.

I ran out and asked him to move, telling him in no uncertain manner that he was blocking the driveway.

He refused to move his car, pointing out to me in very graphic terms that there was no where else for miles around where he could go.

I got no support from the Police Constable, who was directing the crowds, as he said,

"Cars have no right to go across that pavement anyway, the kerb has not been adapted to allow access for vehicles."

So legally I had not a leg to stand on.

I stormed back into the hostel very, very angry.

I had wasted two precious hours watching that space to no avail, so I was angrier with myself than with the car driver. But still I cursed him under my breath and wished him all he had wished me! The front door slammed behind me with an almighty crash.

All the girls, who had been standing around in the hall watching this spectacle, scattered, and ran to their rooms, they did not want to tangle with me when they saw I was angry.

Gordon came and we went to our favourite spot for lunch, with me complaining all the time about 'bad mannered, selfish people' he must have been quite pleased that he could not park his car for long enough to do the work when we got back.

Off he went, hardly waiting until I had got out of the car, saying he would come back another time when there was no football match in progress.

After the match, as I was sitting in my study on the ground floor at the front of the hostel. I watched the crowds of fans pouring out of the ground and up the road, towards Aubert Park and the hostel; I thought,

'I'm missing the wrestling, I must go and watch the wrestling.'

I went to my bedroom at the back of the flat and switched on the television, settling myself down to watch. After a few seconds I realised what I was doing and jumping up said 'What AM I doing? I don't like wrestling, I never watch wrestling'.

At that very moment a bottle hit the front window, showering the chair that I had been sitting on a few minutes before, and the rest of the room, with tiny slivers of glass. I would have been, at best, badly cut, and at worst, been severely injured, if I had not gone out of the room to watch the television!

The Manchester United fans, (for that is who they were,) who had thrown the bottle, then picked up the large piece of wood that was lying in the drive. This wood was used to help the vehicles, (illegally as I now knew,) to mount the kerb. They smashed the windscreen and all the windows, of the car blocking the drive with this block of wood They then proceeded to do the same sort of thing to all the other cars in the area.

I ran round the hostel telling the girls to stay inside and keep the babies away from the windows.

Afraid for them and quaking in my shoes I felt totally appalled by the whole episode.

After all the dreadful things I had wished on that man, and here was his car utterly wrecked! I was thinking, and I was sure he would think, that I had had a large hand in that destruction and I spent the rest of the weekend in abject misery.

At the first opportunity on Monday morning I telephoned Lord Soper, the man who was in overall charge of all the hostels, and blurted out the whole sorry tale. He listened in silence, and then, laughing heartily, he said,

"What are you worrying about, weren't you saved? Weren't you made to leave the dangerous area, and go and switch on your television set? There must be some reason for that, don't you think?

'God works in a mysterious way, his wonders to perform'. Go and get on with your work and stop distressing yourself."

I try very hard not to wish any one any harm now, but it is difficult to control my thoughts all the time.

EVEN BABIES CAN HEAL.

I had been caring for a baby named Emily[2] for four months during my time at the hostel and took her with me wherever I went.

One evening I was invited to supper at Kingsway Hall by some friends who lived and worked there and naturally took her with me.

One of the guests worked in the day centre in the building, and had injured his ankle falling down some steps, a few days previously. He was still finding it difficult to walk unaided by a stick.

After supper when it was time for me to return to the hostel, he offered to carry the child from the forth floor to the street.

I walked behind with the carrycot and all the other things that one needs for an outing with a child.

As I followed him I saw with great amusement that he was walking with no sign of discomfort whatever.

Down in the street the taxi arrived and I climbed in first, he handed the child to me and I smiled and said how good it was to see that his ankle was no longer troubling him.

"What?" he said, "What, oh my goodness, you are right, look I can walk, isn't that fantastic?"

So saying he did a little dance along the pavement, keeping up with the taxi as we drove off.

What does that mean? Did the child have the power to heal even at that early age?

Or was it just that my friend had been given something other than his pain to concentrate on, and had therefore overcome it?

I do not suppose we will ever know the true answer but it certainly gives us food for thought do you not agree?

[2] Not real name

HOW SPIRIT MANAGE TO GET THEIR OWN WAY.

I very often wonder why it is that no one seems to be able to tell me anything about my material, physical, life, such as what to do next, where to aim my sights, and so on. I have consulted some of the well-known mediums, they all say,

"You must work for Spirit. You know you have the gift of healing," Etc, Etc,

I have never been given anything which has been proved to be true about physical/material me.

Not one person has ever given me proof absolute of my seven children who have died, or of the many members of my family who have all died.

I know that it would be difficult for anyone to convince me without absolute proof, such as, names and dates or places, but one would think someone out there could do for me, what has been done for thousands of others through me.

I visited a woman who read the tarot cards in Eastbourne in 1980, but she said nothing that made any sense to me at all.

There were things like "You will be changing your car within three weeks."

"I don't have a car"

"Oh, well, you'll be driving around in a new one within that time."

"I don't drive." Etc; Etc;

This continued for about twenty minutes, her saying, me not able to accept anything she said, until she became exasperated, and throwing the cards in the air she said,

"I don't know what you are doing here. You know much more about this than I do."

I assured her that I knew nothing about the tarot cards. She went on to say,

"Well, it's a pity you weren't here three weeks ago; I needed someone to take over my other rooms, but I've found someone now, if she doesn't stay the course will you take over?"

I told her, "No I'm afraid I can't, I don't use my gifts for money."

"Well then, you are a bigger fool than I thought you were."

"But I believe a gift is given to be given."

"Oh well, that's up to you. Leave me your card there are lots of my clients who visit London and want to see someone while they are there. Whether you charge them or not is up to you, but you are a fool if you don't."

I left her my card and walked away, disappointed once more. I had thought I needed some guidance, some proof that I was, or was not, on the right track, and she had been highly recommended!

Two weeks later she rang me to say that the woman who had taken over her other rooms needed to go on holiday for two weeks, and would I take over for those two weeks?

I had never sat anywhere and said "Here I am, you may come and have a consultation with me." I had always been adamant that NO ONE had the right to do that.

The using and giving of psychic gifts should be the most simple, natural thing in the world, and help and, or, healing should be given where and when it was needed; in the street, on a bus or train, or wherever the need was seen.

However, I spoke about my dilemma with some friends whose opinion I value highly: those who have known me for many years, and watched Spirit at work through me. I begged them to tell me what to do,

"What shall I do, if I go I will have to charge to enable me to cover the rent for the rooms, and I'm sure nothing will come if I'm asking for money!"

"Don't be an idiot all your life. Go on get on with it. You haven't looked for it, or pushed yourself forward, it's fallen into your lap, an opportunity, which, you tell others, that they 'should not let go by!"

John N... a particularly close friend counselled me, reminding me that, "You think nothing of charging for your artwork. That's also a gift, isn't it? Do go and get on with it, you can't put it off for ever!"

So I went, and sat on that first day as I still do every day, praying that no one would come.

"Please God," I said, "Please don't let anyone come. I know nothing will happen, Please, don't let them come."

But - I saw six clients on that first day, and at the end of the day I felt fitter, better, and more alive than I had ever felt in my life.

So I said, "0 K. Sir, if this is what you want me to do, then this is what I will do."

I have been working on recommendations from those that came in those two weeks, and have not had one commission for my artwork, since that day.

A few days after I had returned to London, I received a telephone call from a stranger who announced himself as Hugh.

He said he wanted to apologise, "I came to see you in Eastbourne, and I'm afraid I was very rude to you. I would like to tell you what happened.

When I visited you in your rooms you told me of a line of men in army officer's uniforms who where standing with their fingers on their lips, they were not saying a word of greeting, just standing quietly as though it was necessary to be silent.

You sat for some time with your fingers on your lips, as though you were conveying the importance of the need for silence. You said that you 'knew' that these men had all been in the army with me, and that they had all died in battle. They said nothing, but it was made clear to you by Spirit - that this was the only way you could explain you 'knowing' what had happened.

You told me your interpretation of this scene, but I could not - would not - accept what was said, saying, "If these men WERE friends of mine, they would want to talk to me. They wouldn't just stand there with their fingers on their lips like a line of idiots; they would want to talk damn it! No, I won't accept that." He continued,

"I was then told that I must contact my son as he was badly in need of his father's advice. I began to demur, but was told to be quiet, as there was more to be said on that subject! I did not like it one bit, but, I did shut up. You continued,

"Your son is working in the United States of America, and he needs you to call him, he desperately needs your advice. You must call him on this number,"

I was then given the number where you said I could contact my son, but once again I refused to accept what had been said.

"My son doesn't need my advice, my son NEVER needs anyone's advice. He is in America but you have not given me the right telephone number. You are talking a lot of — — —nonsense, and I'm not going to listen to any more of this."

So saying, I stood up and walked out, refusing to pay for such a load of rubbish.

As I was walking away I shouted back, "I've been to the best sensitive's in the land, and you are certainly not one of them. You never will be any good at all."

Now Hugh was desperate to apologise for his rudeness.

He told me that a short time after he had returned to his home, he received a message asking him to contact his solicitors. He did that, and was told to telephone his son. The solicitor gave Hugh a number where he would reach him - it was not until later that Hugh realised that this was the same number that he had been given in the reading in Eastbourne.

Hugh rang America, his son's first words on hearing his fathers voice were, "Dad, I need your advice."

The young man's Grandmother had left him a house, which he needed to sell, and Hugh had all the papers in England. The sale could not proceed without those papers.

On the morning of the day Hugh telephoned me wanting to

apologise, he'd had an important luncheon appointment.

As he always did, he looked through his visitor's C.V. during the morning. To his great joy he saw that they had both been in the same regiment, and he thought 'Oh, goody, we can chat about the army to break the ice.'

Then, - he saw the picture of me, sitting in my room in Eastbourne, with my fingers on my lips, and later, telling him of the row of silent army officers. He decided to find something else to talk about, something else they had in common, just as a precaution you understand, just in case there was some reason for such a ridiculous message!

As Hugh continued reading the C.V. he found that their sons had followed the same academic path, so decided on that topic as an 'Ice breaker.' The lunch meeting was very successful, Hugh had his contracts signed and his visitor was quite satisfied with the way things had been completed. The two of them retired to Hugh's club to celebrate. A colleague of Hugh's joined them after a while, and being an ex army man, as ex army men do, (If they haven't been to the best clairvoyant in the land.) he started talking about his time in the army during the war.

Hugh's visitor jumped to his feet, and while picking up his briefcase, said menacingly, "Don't talk to me about the war, or the army, anyone who talks to me about the army is in imminent danger of having his teeth knocked out!"

And with that he stormed out of the club."

So you can see that if Hugh had done what he intended in the first instance, and started a conversation about their belonging to the same regiment, he would never have got very far with the meeting, or had the contracts safely signed and sealed. The memory of his reading with me had been most important, even if he had not understood what was meant at the time. Needless to say he sent my fee and has been to see me many times since.

As I was on my way home at the end or my two weeks 'stand-in' stint, the artist who drew portraits of the people on the pier stopped me and said.

"I've just had a client of yours in here."

"How do you know it was a client of mine?"

"Because she couldn't stop talking about you. It was as much as I could do to keep her still long enough to draw her at all, she was so excited, no, not excited, - amazed? Yes, that's the right word, amazed. She said you had told her that her son, who had been killed a few months ago, was there with you, and that her husband, who was also dead, had come with his son and shown himself to you.

Her husband had come with the son to show how alike they were. Her son told you where and how he had been killed. They also told you to tell her the make, and number of the car in which the boy died! You then said that you could see the street where the accident happened, and you gave her the name of it.

But, the thing she found most difficult to understand was that you described her garden in minute detail, and told her that she had a five-bar gate!

She kept repeating, 'How did she know I have a five-bar gate? How did she know what plants are in my garden?' I tell you Selena I don't want too many of your clients in here, it's too spooky'."

I said I was sorry he had found it all so disturbing and suggested that perhaps he should come for a reading, free of charge of course, then he would see that there really was nothing remotely 'spooky' about it. He declined my offer saying,

"No thanks, there's too much truth said there for my liking!"

I went home quite concerned and puzzled, not because the photographer had declined my offer of a reading, but over my client's strange reaction to what had been said.

She had been given details of her son's recent death, the make and number of the car, so many details, and yet the only thing that she found amazing was that I knew about her plants and the five-bar gate.

This information seemed to mean more to her than the return from the dead of her husband and her recently killed son! Why? I asked myself. Why?

Then I saw as clear as day why. She was right to wonder at just that. All the other things she had been told about were still fresh in her mind, her son's death, the loss of her husband, indeed she thought about them constantly, and they could have been plucked from there by telepathy. But the garden and the five-bar gate? No, nothing was further from her mind.

So, does this prove that there is not only such a thing as life after death, but that they also know what is happening to us at any given time? I have reached the conclusion that this seems to be the only answer.

Barbara C. was another person who came to see me during those two weeks. Barbara was an hotelier, and in the course of her reading she was told about her son-in-law John, who, she was told, was not pulling his weight in the hotel. The reasons for this were described in detail, and this seemed to satisfy her.

I then started to talk about her grandchild, the child's aspirations, and dreams, and where she (the child) should concentrate her energies. Whilst talking about this child I started to cry. NO, I wept. I wept copious tears.

Barbara became most upset and said, "Don't you tell me something is going to happen to my grandchild."

She was told, "No, no my dear, nothing is going to happen to your grandchild, but in two weeks all will be changed." This was repeated three times, "In two weeks all will be changed."

She was then told that on a certain date, the date was given, someone would come who would be of great financial assistance to her, and help her to run her hotel.

Barbara had been getting more and more uneasy as the reading went on. At that last statement she stood, drew herself up to a great height, and as she walked out of the door turned and said, "My son-in-law helps me run my hotel, and I don't need any ones financial assistance, thank you very much."

Once again, weeks after I had returned to London, I had a telephone from her to tell me that two weeks to the day after she had been to see me, her son-in-law had died, so all was indeed changed, and of course, her grandchild wept.

A few weeks after the funeral of John, her son in law, an old friend she had not seen for many years; (and with whom she had had no contact since she had married,) turned up by sheer chance on the steps of the hotel!

Sheer chance? Coincidence? luck? or a greater hand at work? He has since been of great financial assistance to her, and is now helping her run her hotel. There must be at least three hundred hotels in that particular resort, yet he had chosen to go to the one owned by my client.

Why did he choose that one? When Barbara asked, "Why?" he said "I have no idea, I just found myself walking this way, and up the steps to your door!"

Barbara wrote to me enclosing my fee, and offering me accommodation, free of charge, in the Hotel if I would go and 'read' for her friends who had not been able to get in to see me during the two weeks I had been in Eastbourne.

She returned to my rooms four years later bringing a friend in need of a reading, and wrote in the 'comments book'

"In 1980 t'was said to me, in two weeks time a change there would be, and so there was, and all came true. So Selena dear, my thanks to you."

Barbara told me that even though she 'thought' she had totally dismissed everything said in the reading; she must have been being made aware subconsciously that something was about to happen, because when her son-in-law had died she was not nearly as upset as she thought she would be!

SEEING THINGS AS THEY ARE HAPPENING

By this time there were so many people who wanted to consult me, that I signed a yearly tenancy on a consulting room in London, charging just enough for readings to pay the rent and overheads. I was working in a semi-trance state now. One day I came back from wherever it is I go when I am working, to find my client, Norah, slumped in the chair, looking shell-shocked.

"What is it?" I asked, "What has happened."

"Don't you know? Don't you remember what you have just told me?"

"Now Norah, you know I never remember what's been said in a reading, you should know you've been here enough times. From the look of you, you had better tell me what happened."

"You told me that my president has been assassinated."

"What! Oh, don't be silly! We don't have a president, we have the Royal Family."

"But I wasn't born here in England, didn't I tell you? I'm Egyptian."

"Ah, well then you do have a president, but I'm sure you must have misheard what was said. If it had happened it would be in the newspapers or on the radio. Something as important as that would be plastered across the front page."

"But I haven't seen a paper today, or listened to the radio."

"I have this morning's 'Daily Mail' and there really is nothing about anyone being assassinated!"

"But truly Selena, that's what you said. Listen to the tape. Please, listen to the tape."

I always make tape recordings of readings for clients to take away. Human nature being what it is, most people remember only what they wanted to hear. If what is said is NOT what they wanted to hear they very rarely remember anything at all.

We turned the tape back to the beginning and there was a very quiet voice saying that Norah would soon be required to visit her mother, who was now living in Greece. Norah must be very gentle with her, as she was not as well as she could be. She would recover, but was in need of some gentle tenderness now. Then - silence for while until—

"You know, of course, that your president is being assassinated."

This from a very loud voice booming in.

"No, Oh no, it can't be." Norah's shocked voice.

"It is so, many people hurt - soldiers running - so many loud explosions."

"Is he alive?"

"Just a minute." Silence again, a long pause this time, then -

"The helicopters are coming. He is being carried into the helicopter. He will not survive - oh my poor face."

End of tape.

By this time, I was also in a state of shock. I said how sorry I was that she had had such an experience.

"Come along, I'll take you for a cup of coffee. We must both try and forget this, it really must be a trick, or a mistake."

As we were leaving, the two young men who ran a shop just along the arcade asked if there was anything they could do, as we both looked ashen. I told them what had been said, and they also insisted that if such a thing had happened it would have been in the newspapers, or reported on the radio.

They had been listening to the radio all the morning and there had been no reports of any assassinations.

Norah and I drank our coffee and I called a taxi for her and sent her home.

I went back to my room, locked the door and refused to see any clients.

I sat in my room and prayed. I desperately needed to know the truth, has this act of barbarism been enacted already? Or it is to be? Or it someone playing dirty tricks? I sat; hoping and praying that President Sadat was safe.

He was achieving so much I longed to be told that, indeed it was a false Spirit message, and yet I dreaded to have that answer because it would mean that neither my clients, nor I were as protected, as we should be. Before each reading I ask that "'the client be given the truth, and that they have the answers they need, rather than those that they want. But thy will, not mine, be done."

But if this sort of thing can happen where is our protection?

An hour later, the young men from the shop, the one's Norah and I had spoken to on our way to the coffee shop, came banging on the door of my room; they were shouting. Shouting so loudly.

"What you said has happened, Selena, it was as you said. It has just been reported on the radio. President Sadat has been murdered."

I do not like listening to the tapes that I make of the readings for my clients, because I do not want to know what has been said. This is mainly because most of my clients want to come back at some time, and if I remembered what had been said, my own interpretations of a situation may interfere with subsequent psychic messages. Neither do I wish to have all the worries of the world on my shoulders. As I surely would have, if I DID remember what was on some of the tapes.

I had agreed to listen to the tape this time because Norah had been so distressed.

I felt very depressed that what had been said had been the truth, but mightily relieved at the same time.

The whole experience was amazing, for Spirit to come WHILST the drama was unfolding had not happened before. Not to me, or, to any one else as far as I knew.

OPPORTUNITIES THAT SLIP OUT OF TIME.

I have let many opportunities slip out of time, and I feel ashamed of myself sometimes when I hear myself telling others how much we miss out when we do this. In the middle seventies I was offered a beautiful Dower House in Kent, the owner Lord W. was asking for a rent of just £50 a year.

'The Dower House' had not been lived in regularly for fifteen years. As the younger members of the Lord W's family had grown up and married, they had stayed there for short periods of time while they were waiting for contracts on their own houses to be completed, but the house had not benefited from a regular occupant.

Lord W. now wanted someone to love and live permanently in, the property.

He was looking for the right person, someone who would bring the house and gardens back to their former glory. The letting agents were asking for £20,000 to be spent on the house over a period of twenty years, which explained why the rent was so low.

I made the journey from London by train, and then, as there were no buses, by taxi: to see the house. I knew immediately that I must have it. I knew every nook and cranny; I knew where each door would lead me, and exactly what I would find there.

In the Dower House were six bedrooms, lots of attics, four reception rooms, a butler's pantry, dairies, stables, two kitchens, a very large one, and a smaller one along the passage. Enough room to fulfil my lifelong dream, a dream in which I have a gracious house: a house large enough to accommodate a resident healer, an acupuncturist, and as many patients as it's possible to fit in, in comfort.

The gardens, almost an acre, had been lovingly laid out many years previously, and were now overgrown and neglected. A herb garden could be seen quite clearly peeping through the overgrowth! I had been learning a considerable amount about herbs and their healing properties over the years and I felt I was now ready to put that knowledge into practice.

Here was my chance to do just that, sitting waiting for me to move in and get on with it! My builder Jeremy agreed to look at the property, to see what was going to need doing, if anything, to make it wind and weatherproof.

This figure of £20,000 that the letting agents were quoting made me slightly nervous! SLIGHTLY? No, VERY nervous.

The house was just what I had wanted for years, and if it was wind and weatherproof, I could not see why it should need so much spending on it. I learned later that the agents wanted the bathrooms modernised and full central heating installed.

The main bathroom was superb as it was as far as I was concerned. The bathtub stretched so far, it was possible to lie flat in it and not touch the end. This spacious bathtub, had mahogany panels, and big brass taps with a splendid shower attachment, they only needed a lot of 'elbow grease' to bring them back to their former glory.

To get into this glorious bath tub one climbed three curved mahogany steps which had a banister to help one on ones way, quite like a short library ladder, but fixed to the side of the tub. Exactly right just as it was.

Central heating was certainly not on my list of priorities, there were large fireplaces in all the rooms. Being a romantic and not thinking about how impracticable it would be, I imagined apple or pine log fires roaring away in all of them, keeping the house warm, perfumed, and comfortable.

I retraced my steps to London full of hope and plans for the future. Jeremy promised he would drive me down to Kent the next weekend and inspect the property. During that preceding week I saw a number of clients, including Noleen, who had started as a client and had become a close friend.

Before her reading, we had a cup of tea and I told her of the Dower House and how much I wanted to fulfil my dreams and plans for it, 'if' it was right for me to do so.

In the course of Noleen's reading, unknown to me, she asked,

"Is it right for Selena to take on the responsibility of such a gigantic project?"

"Yes. Yes she must do it. It is right for her now. There is a strip of land, ten feet wide, this piece of ground is between two walls, and must be made into a Japanese water garden. People will come from all over the world to see this, and that way she can pay her bills. There is also a piano which has to be rescued."

"Is the piano in the house?"

"No, it has been whooshed out, it's been whooshed out, and we want it taken back into the house."

There was then quite a long silence, and then another voice came in and said,

"She must change her solicitor; tell her she MUST change her solicitor now before it's too late, and she loses everything."

A tape was running for the reading and for the second time, I was encouraged to listen to a client's reading!

Jeremy and I travelled to Kent in his car, the following Sunday, and on the way, I told him of what had been said in Noleen's reading. He was faintly amused, but said he could not believe in that sort of thing.

I also had my doubts by this time. I had been thinking about the statements made on the tape.

When I had made a thorough inspection of the house and grounds, I certainly had not seen a strip of land between two walls, or caught as much as a glimpse of a piano!

We arrived at the house; Jeremy looked at it and proclaimed the structure and roof sound. Only minor repairs were needed to window frames and doors, and a bit of plastering here and there. We decided to examine the grounds and log what sort of plants and trees there were, and see how many could be saved.

We came to the boundary, and I was trying to identify a shrub which climbed the wall, when to my surprise the wall ended - I looked round the end of it, and - there was another wall running parallel, a strip of land ten feet wide, ran between.

We stood as though rooted to the spot. Both of us were shocked at this discovery, I do not know if my face was as white as his was, if so, I must have looked horrible! He gave himself a shake and said,

"Well, there's your strip of land, I'm off to find the piano."

Still badly shaken, but managing a faint smile I continued to log the trees and bushes, and found some fruit to take back to Canterbury for my daughters. I was going to visit them later, and show them the details of the house, before making the journey back to London. I was putting the fruit in Jeremy's car, when I heard his voice; it sounded very far away.

"Please come here, Selena, please come here. I want to show you something."

"Where are you?"

"By the stables."

I went and found him standing by, and hanging on to, one of the stable doors.

"What is it?" I asked.

"I think you'd better look in there." He said quietly, pointing into the stable.

"Why?"

"Please, just look."

I thought he had found something that was going to take the £20,000 to put right, and I hesitated.

"Go on, it's all right, please look."

I plucked up my courage, and peeping through my fingers into the stable I saw to my astonishment, that there in the middle of the cobbled floor was a baby grand piano, covered in cobwebs and dust but it seemed to be all in one piece.

When we regained our composure, we walked slowly to the car and got in.

We sat in the car for some time, trying to come to terms with the fact that we had been privileged to have been given such extraordinary evidence of the truth of Noleen's reading.

Jeremy and I then drove to Canterbury to extol the virtues of the place to my daughter Michelle, who spent the next few hours trying to talk me out of taking the house and, as she saw it, "all it's attendant problems!"

"What if you are ill again?"

"You have no transport, and there is no station for miles."

"Suppose the builder is wrong, and the house falls down round your ears?" and so on - and so on. —-

Simply being sensible of course, and trying to make me see how irresponsible she thought I was! All she said was perfectly true. But I was 'pretty' sure that I SHOULD have the place, and that God would provide for my needs. He always has - hasn't he?

This time however, with something this gigantic, I felt I needed some moral support. Michelle refused to come and see the house, not wanting to encourage me to make any foolish decisions.

Nessa was out with a friend, so I could not get her to back me up. Having got no support, after a while, I too began to have my doubts about the wisdom of my plans!

The agents with whom I was negotiating for 'Peg's Stores' a small shop nearby my flat in London, had recommended a solicitor, Mr Abbey* in Piccadilly. (*Not real name.)

I instructed him to get all the necessary papers from Lord W's, agents and draw up contracts for both properties. The weeks went by, I was busy seeing clients and whenever I telephoned Mr A. he said a variation of,

"Yes all is well, I am in constant contact with Lord W's-agent, and the estate agents, and contracts are being drawn up. I am quite happy with the way things are progressing."

I did nothing to check that what he was telling me was right, I was seeing clients most of the time and very busy so I took his word for it. I was getting no support for my plans from my daughters, and I wondered if natural law was also against me as everything seemed to be taking such an age.

I knew my daughters would have my interests at heart - perhaps I should listen to them and put my dreams away!

After many weeks of waiting and Mr A's procrastinating, I finally saw how stupid I was being, and knew if I wasn't careful I would miss the opportunities that had been put my way.

I decided to take charge of things myself. I had telephoned Mr A. and got no satisfactory answers to any of my questions, so I instructed him to send me every paper concerning both properties, details of calls made, copies of letters written or received. I told him very firmly,

"I want all these papers on my breakfast tray tomorrow morning."

The envelope arrived; the only papers in it were the ones I had handed him two months earlier! He had done precisely nothing. I lost both properties.

He has never had the nerve to send me a bill, you can imagine what I would have said if he had!

My own fault of course, I should have obeyed my own intuitions, (and Noleen's reading,) and done something about both properties myself. Not asked for, or expected, support from anyone.

I had KNOWN the house was right when I first saw it, what more could I ask?

I had not listened, and I had not changed my solicitor either. Noleen was extremely angry with me. She said,

"How can you expect us to do what you say, if YOU don't do what you are so clearly shown to do? I no longer have any faith in you, and will not come here again."

I have not seen Noleen, or the Dower House, since! 'Peg's Stores' was let to someone else as the agents had heard nothing from Mr Abbey, and turned into a snack bar.

MORE UNBIDDEN MESSAGES.

I have been a regular customer in my favourite Fish restaurant, 'Geales' in Farmer Street. Notting Hill Gate, for fifteen years. But in all that time have only been there twice in daylight hours.

It was on the last of these occasions that a most disconcerting thing happened. I had finished my lunch, and was wondering why I was there. I had not been hungry and I very seldom eat a big meal in the middle of the day.

Whilst I was musing thus, I felt the presence of someone standing by my side. I could not see this person you understand, but knew without a doubt that this 'being' was a woman.

How did I KNOW? I am afraid I can not explain that, I just knew. I also knew that she was telling me her name was 'Marion'.

She had been 'dead' but a few days and did not want to leave the earth until she had cleared up a few things that were troubling her, and her friends.

She insisted that I go over to five people sitting in the other part of the restaurant and tell them she was there in the restaurant, and that it had been an accident, she had not meant to kill herself!

I sat arguing with this person who was impinging herself on my mind, I was saying to her,

"I can not go over to five complete strangers who are eating their lunch and say, 'Marion is here, and she asks me to tell you that she did not mean to kill herself.' They will think I am, at best drunk, and at worst mad!"

I tried to get up from my chair, as I had every intention of leaving, but I could not move from my seat.

I was surrounded by an almost overwhelming smell of flowers and plants and it was obvious that she must have brought this in with her, as there were none in the restaurant. Again I heard the words pleading with me,

"Please, you must tell them It WAS an accident - Please, you must."

There was no point in arguing any longer, and I reluctantly agreed to go and talk to them. I was immediately released from my chair and walked slowly over to their table. I stood there, clenching and unclenching my hands. The five people sitting there stared at me with some annoyance for intruding on their privacy.

"Excuse me." I said, "Please, excuse me." Five pairs of eyes were turned my way.

The man nearest me said. "Well, What is it?"

"I'm very sorry to intrude, but" —- I could say no more, words failed me.

"Then why are you intruding?"

"Do you know some one named Marion?"

Five very shocked, white faces, mouths open, looked at me as though they could not believe what I had just said.

"We have just come from her funeral. Why do you ask a question like that?"

"Because she is here."

Five amazed faces began to look around in disbelief.

Silence for a while as I tried to pull myself together and gather enough courage to relay Marion's message.

I took a deep breath, and decided to ignore the consequences and tell them what I had been impressed to say.

"Marion says that she did not mean to kill herself, it was an accident: I don't know what she means, but she refused to go, or allow me to go home, until I came here and told you."

Deep sighs came from the five at the table, then the man said,

"You were right to come and talk to us. It is being said that Marion committed suicide by taking an overdose of a sleeping draft. We could not believe this of her, but that is what people are saying."

This reply gave me the courage to continue,

"Oh, well then, were there a lot of flowers at her funeral?" I asked, and went onto say, "She brought an overwhelming smell of flowers in with her."

Five smiling, faces!

"No, there were no flowers or plants." Seeing my confusion the man continued, "The person you are speaking of owned a florist's shop just round the corner from here. She specifically asked that there should be no flowers."

One of the others said, "Thank you for talking to us, you have given us some comfort. It must have been difficult for you to accost five complete strangers! How do you know that what you feel is the truth? That you are not fooling yourself, or worse, that someone else is not fooling you?"

"Oh, that's easy, whenever I am made aware in 'that' way it is always truth - that is not the problem, there is always someone there who will understand what is being said. It's getting me to say it that's the problem!"

We had a drink together to toast Marion, and I went home, happy in the knowledge that five people knew the truth about Marion's death, and Marion was free to go on.

EXPERIENCE MUST COME BEFORE KNOWLEDGE.

When people meet me for the first time, they are quite often sceptical of the things I do and say. The 'knowledge' is not something we understand that easily, unless we have some proof of our own to use as a measure.

I will rarely accept anything unless it can be proved beyond a doubt, and will never ask anyone else to accept things blindly. None of us can know, until we know, that sounds obvious does it not?

But - please think about it for a few seconds.

No one can know what it is like to be in any situation unless they have been in that situation themselves. They may think they know, because they have spent God knows how many years studying, and yes they may know intellectually, but they can not KNOW.

No midwife can KNOW what it is like to give birth to a child if she/he has not given birth. They CAN know the mechanic's, like what happens and when, but not what the actual birth pains are like.

Likewise a Doctor, he/she can not know HOW a patient feels unless that have had that particular illness.

Many of us think we know what we would have done, would do, in any given situation, but, we can only know if we have been there ourselves. I thought I knew what I would do if I was ever in a car smash. I'd be the hero, stay calm and help those who needed it. What did I do when I was involved in a pile-up?   I sat there in the back of the car screaming my head off, some hero. So you see one has to have been there to know.

I am pretty certain that this is why most genuine mediums have a fairly tough life. They must have had the same experience as the people they are trying to help. That's why most of us CAN say,

"I know how you feel, I've been there."

In other words we have to KNOW how it feels, and to have been there, before we can really help someone else!

WORKING FULL-TIME.

During 1983 I was again in Eastbourne seeing clients, having taken the advice I'd been given, and was now working full time as a Medium.

I had been concerned about Nessa all day, and had tried to telephone her at her home. No reply. I thought she might be with her sister, and also tried there. No reply.

"Well," I said to myself, "Maybe she is at my flat." But no answer from there either. I rang one after the other for hours on end, and still had no reply from any of the numbers. I knew, somehow, I knew, that she was in a hospital, but I did NOT know which hospital.

Can I hear you saying, "What's the point of that? There's not much point in knowing that she is in a hospital if you don't know which one, is there?"

And you are quite right. But it was me who was at fault, not 'The Management.' I was worrying, using my conscious mind, instead of sitting quietly and listening.

Nessa had not been well for some time and I had visited her the day before I returned to Eastbourne. She had not mentioned any thing about having to go into hospital, but I rang the hospital where she had been treated as an outpatient and asked about admissions. I was told, "No, she is not here."

I tried all the hospitals in North London and each time received a negative answer. Her name was not on any admission slip, yet I was still sure she was in hospital somewhere.

I went to see Peter, a friend of mine. It was eleven o'clock at night by this time so there was no possibility of my getting back to London today.

He said "Go home and go to bed, you have people to see tomorrow who need you and you need your sleep so you must go to bed."

I had seven appointments the next day, including, at lunchtime, two ladies for healing. I slept fitfully and in the morning I went to my rooms, but I could not work.

The ladies came for their appointments at mid-day and I sat chatting to them in the waiting room, trying to put off the healing sessions for as long as I could, hoping that Ness would manage to let me know where she was.

Eventually, they looked at me and said, "We will have to go soon. We told the hotel we would be back for lunch, and we would like some healing, please."

I said "OK. I will just go and get some water."

Clients are always given a glass of water after healing. I went into the cloakroom and stood, mentally asking Nessa to contact me and let me know where she was, and that she was all right. I felt someone taking hold of my hand, and I clearly heard Nessa's voice saying,

"Come on now, let's get on with some work shall we?"

I knew then the most important thing I could do for Nessa was to do just that. Wherever she was, whatever had happened, she wanted me to see the people who were in need. I went back to my rooms and said,

"Right, come along ladies, let's get on with your healing."

I saw the rest of my clients that day, locked up, then caught a train to London, arriving in Victoria at about ten forty p.m. and took a taxi to Nessa's flat in North London.

On the journey across London the taxi driver noticed that I looked very worried and asked,

"Is there anything I can do, love?"

I told him of my experiences that morning, and by the time we arrived at her flat, he was as concerned as I was.

He insisted on coming round to the flat with me instead of leaving me in the street. The flat was in total darkness, which was not surprising as it was almost midnight by this time. I rang the bell a number of times and knocked on the door, trying not to make too much noise considering the time. The driver kept a large flashlight in his taxi and he had brought this with him. He shone it through the bedroom window.

Her room and bed were empty. The window was open, and her cats were wandering around crying. I was sure that she would not leave her cats unattended and a window open, unless something drastic had happened.

The taxi driver helped me to climb through the window. She was not there. I wandered around the flat with the flashlight. No, it did not occur to me to switch on the light.

The cats came to me, crying for food. I fed them and then remembered that the taxi driver was still outside. I told him to come in through the window. He said,

"What's wrong with coming in through the door?"

I had not thought of opening the door. Nessa does not like people going into her flat unless she invites them, and I felt that even I was invading her privacy by being there. I let him in reluctantly, knowing I could not leave him outside, but aware of how Nessa would feel.

We glanced round the flat to see if we could find anything to say where she was, not wanting to look at her papers or open any drawers.

A note to a neighbour or to me perhaps? I really had no idea what I was looking for. What I expected to find, I did not know either.

There was absolutely nothing. We were just about to leave when the driver pointed to a sheet of paper on the floor.

It had not been there when I let the taxi driver in but it was there now, in the middle of the floor in her living room. He picked it up and gave it to me,

I was going to put it on her desk, not wanting to read her papers, but then I noticed that it was hospital headed notepaper. I still felt I should not read her letters and asked him to read it. It was a letter dated two days previously, telling her she must be at the hospital on Wednesday afternoon. Today was Thursday. This would explain why I had known she was in hospital yesterday.

But, I had telephoned all of them and been told 'No, she is not here.' I telephoned the number on the letter. They still insisted 'there is no one of that name here.'

The taxi driver said, "Come on, let's go and find out what's happening."

We drove with the letter to the hospital. The receptionist looked through the admissions for Wednesday, and again said,

"No, there is no one here of that name."

I showed him the letter. He said that it made no difference, there was no one in the hospital with that name.

Then a quick, bright flash of light drew my attention to a box on the shelf on the other side of his little cubicle.

"How about over there?" I said.

"But those are not admissions", he replied.

"Please, please look. I must find her." He saw how important it was to me and agreed. He looked in the box, and her card was there, saying she had been admitted yesterday and was in the Surgical Ward.

I suggested that he telephone the ward to see if she was all right. He rang and spoke to the Sister who informed him that she had had a bone biopsy around midday and was now sleeping.

He gave me this information and I felt a great wave of relief sweep through me and said,

"OK. Mr. Taxi Man, you can take me home now."

He drove me back to Kensington and came in for a drink to warm him up as we had got quite cold wandering about, and there was no more work that he could do that night, as it was then two o'clock.

We sat and talked for some time and we decided that someone must have been on my side to make him the first in the taxi line up outside Victoria Station!

He was absolutely marvellous. He could have dropped me off at Nessa's flat, or said at any time that he had had enough of running around for me, but he would not give up until we found her, and he had got me home again. I have looked for him since, but have not seen him. I did not take his name but if he reads this I hope he will contact me. I would like to thank him.

When Nessa had taken my hand as I was getting the glass of water for my clients earlier that day, she had been under Anaesthetic and in the operating theatre.

This had allowed her to leave her physical body in safe hands while she came to reassure me.

She had seen that I was worried and had come to try and tell me what was happening to her.

I was not listening well enough if I had been I would have known there was no need for my concern.

Our Spirit can willingly leave our body when we are asleep and travel great distances to guide or comfort other people who are in need. It remains attached to our body and returns before we wake. It is only in death that the 'Spirit' becomes severed from the body.

I asked her later why she had not let me know she was going into hospital when I had spoken to her on the Wednesday morning and she said it was because she did not want to worry me.

She had known I had a number of people to see and wanted me to get on with my work rather than spend time visiting her when her decision as to whether or not to have the operation was to be a last-minute one anyway.

"But if you had told me, I COULD have got on with my work. I wouldn't have been so distraught at not being able to find you." I grumbled selfishly.

She had been very sick for weeks before, and had not been eating properly; so I naturally feared the worst, as we all do. Will I never learn to listen quietly?

The reason I had not been able to contact Michelle was that she had been out with friends until very late on the Wednesday evening. She also had a very early start in a new 'voluntary-work' job at a school nearby which she had undertaken to start the following morning.

After I assured myself all was well with Nessa and Michelle, I returned to Eastbourne to get on with my work which had been piling up for a couple of days.

A PRAYER GIVEN BY SPIRIT FOR USE IN READINGS

The following prayer was quoted for the first time during a reading. Where it came from I do not know, but it has since been used in readings quite often, with minor changes to cover what each client needs at the time.

> "Divine one touch with thy love
> the mantle of this earth,
> which is woe,
> Transform its tatters with thy magic.
> Oh Divine one,
> Dearest God, listen.
> Let thy brightness creep the shadows.
> Make the midnight shine with thy countenance.
> Divine one, make love, earth's armour, strong:
> That it shall turn the blade of woe.
> Make these pleadings blessed with thy listening.
> Amen."

For the client, Michael W, who had come straight from a conference meeting, it was changed thus:

'Make love earth's armour, strong, and bring peace to the world. But let each man know that peace is his responsibility, and his alone. It has nothing to do with governments, trade unions, or anyone else in power; it has to do with each and every one of us individually.'

Michael W. told me that in a business meeting, before he came to me, he and his colleagues had all been trying to blame everyone else for the state of the world so those words were just what he needed to take back to the meeting!!

In his reading he was also told that he was 'swinging the lead' by coming for a reading with me, because he should have been attending a trade union meeting at that time. But it was necessary for him to hear that prayer, and to be told other things about his life, before he went back to the conference hall.

He told me afterwards that, yes, he was indeed 'swinging the lead' he had slipped out of a meeting, having made up his mind that if I could see him, it would be right and he would get the answers he needed. If I could not see him, he would take that as a sign that he had to work things out for himself.

In the reading, he'd had proof of survival, and his life had been sorted out. Many things were talked about that he had not brought into his conscious mind, but which must have been in his sub-conscious, because he recognised them and saw that, of course, the way shown that afternoon was the only way he could go.

"THE MANAGEMENT'S" HELP IN A SEA RESCUE

The day was hot and sunny and I lay on my sun-bed on the pier. I had no appointments until mid-day and was enjoying the sun. Many people came and asked me to do a reading for them. I refused them all saying,

"No, I am going to sit in the sun. I'm not seeing anyone."

The girl who made my appointments for me was shocked at my behaviour, as she knew the rent had to be paid, and we did not have enough to pay half of it.

"What are you doing? These people need to see you. Come on now, get on with some work."

I insisted that I was going to stay in the sun, thinking I was being very selfish in wanting something for myself. I had got out my sun-bed, and put on my shorts, and I lay there thoroughly enjoying myself. My twelve o-clock appointment arrived, and I told her to go away and come back in an hour or so.

She was quite cross, as she had made a great effort to be there on time. But I was adamant, so she went to get some lunch before, instead of after, the reading, grumbling about how inconsiderate 'some people' were.

I just smiled at her and sent her on her way, wondering all the time why I was behaving in such an outrageous way, and feeling quite guilty about it all, but unable to act according to my conscience.

I knew why a few minutes later, when I heard a child's voice shouting

"Help, help, there's a kid in the sea. Help somebody do something!"

I raced down to the lower pier, taking the steps two at a time, and there under the bottom platform - ten feet below where I was standing - was a boy in the sea struggling to hold on to one of a number of the iron girders that supported the pier. He was having great difficulty because they were covered with encrustation's which had accumulated over the years.

Another boy was trying to reach him, but could not do so because the boy, and the churning sea, lay four feet below the broken concrete slabs on which he was trying desperately to keep his balance. The boy in the sea was too far away, and the little 'would-be' rescuer's arms were just not long enough to reach his friend, and both of them were becoming desperate. The one struggling in the sea was being cut and scratched, trying to hold on to the iron girders, and was losing his strength to fight the waves.

Fishermen went on fishing - women went on knitting - and my assistant continued to read her book. NONE of them had heard the child's voice shouting, "HELP ME, WON'T SOMEONE PLEASE HELP ME!"

Not one person looked up. No one moved - it was as though they were all in a film that had been stopped.

I grabbed one of the fishermen and said "Do something, for goodness sake, do something."

"Do something about what?" he snarled.

"That child, there, in the sea. Look, can't you see that boy down there? Go and get him out."

I pointed in the direction of the exhausted, and by now, scarcely struggling child.

The man called one of his fishermen friends, and together they went down the broken steps leading to what had been the lower platform, before the ravages of time and the sea had taken their toll. The man I had grabbed so unceremoniously lay on the slabs hanging on to the other man's feet while he leaned over the edge of the platform. Together they managed to pull the child up and out of the sea. Handing him over to me, they resumed their fishing!

The rescued boy told me his name was Kevin and his 'would-be' rescuer's name was Carl. I took Kevin upstairs to the deck hand's rest room. I told him to take off his wet clothes and sit under the hand drier, which was on the wall above some seating, while I went to try and locate one of the deck staff to find out where they kept the first aid equipment and towels.

There were none. Commandeering a large banqueting cloth from the restaurant, I took it back to where Kevin was drying out, and told him to wrap himself in it.

Later when we took the things from his jeans pockets, so that I could rinse the jeans before sending them to be dried, we found a penknife, a return ticket for the journey home, some money, and a rabbit's foot.

Picking up the rabbit's foot, one of the deck hands said "Well, that didn't do you much good did it?"

Kevin looked at him scathingly, and said,

"I'm 'ere ain't I?"

I smiled to myself and went over to the window to call Carl. He was waiting anxiously down on the pier to know how Kevin was. I told him to come up and get Kevin's clothes, take them to the launderette and get them dry.

Kevin's mother had taught him to swim. She had also told him.

"If you ever get out of your depth, or find yourself in difficulties, swim for your life, and shout like hell. Make as much noise as you can!"

He told me how proud he was of his mum, and made me promise not to tell her of his morning's adventure.

"She mustn't know, she'd kill me for being so stupid." He said.

He had known the bottom platform was dangerous and that it had been closed off for years. It had continued to disintegrate during that time, but Kevin had gone down there to recover some precious fishing line which had got itself tangled up with the girders. As he was tugging at the line his shoe came off, and plop into the sea it went. Kevin knew he could not go home without a shoe, if he wanted to stay alive, so he stretched down to try and get it from the sea. As he stretched and reached for his shoe he lost his balance and went tumbling down into the sea. There he had remained kicking and struggling to get back to the surface, then sinking again trying desperately to cling on to those treacherous girders, but less and less successfully, until I heard that voice and grabbed the fisherman.

Kevin and I talked until Carl came back with his now dry clothes. They both began to get very excited about what heroes they would be when they went back to school and told the other boys about Kevin's rescue.

I said that if I heard they had made heroes of themselves, they would have me to answer to; they were not heroes, they were very silly boys, and Kevin was lucky to be alive. I sent them home, with Kevin none the worse for his adventure except for his cuts and bruises.

If I had been working when he fell into the sea, my doors would have been tightly closed and I would not have heard the boy's cries for help. No one else had heard a sound. My assistant said,

"I wondered what you were doing when you raced down those steps. I thought to myself, what's she up to now? She's probably going to tell those poor kids off for something or other; she is in a strange mood today."

I spoke to many people on the pier. No one had heard anything other than the normal sounds of children playing and grown-ups chattering. I went back to my rooms, saw my postponed twelve o'clock appointment and everyone else who wanted to come.

I worked through until almost mid-night, making up for my morning in the sun!

Kevin came in to see me two days later bringing his father, and a new fishing rod his father had bought him. Kevin had caught his first fish with his new rod and line, and offered it to me as a thank you. I refused his gift as graciously as I could, as the poor thing was still alive and squirming!

Carl and his friends call in whenever they are on the pier to say 'hello' and sometimes to talk about the herbs which I have growing in the shop. They want to know what they are used for, and how much to use. It pleases me that they see me as a 'normal' person and not someone who is pointed out as 'The fortune-teller' or worse,

'The one who'll cast a spell on you if you're not careful!'

I have heard so many parents say this as the children crowd round the door of the shop wanting to know where the wonderful smells are coming from. The smell of the herbs and potpourri often escapes in the summer when the shop door is open. My shop was called, 'Herbs, Honey, and Holograms.'

I sold horoscopes and had put some of these on a rack outside the window, so that people could select whichever ones they wanted. A tin, with a hole in the lid, was on a chair underneath the rack. Attached to the chair was a large notice inviting clients to

'Please put money for horoscopes in here, 30 pence each. Thank you.'

I sat in the shop one day and watched as an elderly couple selected the horoscopes they wanted; carefully looking at the dates to make sure they had the right ones for all the family.

I smiled, thinking how pleased they would all be when they received them.

The woman searched through her purse for the money to put in the tin, only to find that the smallest she had was a five-pound note. I was just about to go out and offer to change a note for her when her husband said,

"Why don't you just take them, there's no-one here to take the money, how will she ever know who took them?"

The woman answered quick as a flash, "Not from one of these I ain't, she might put a spell on me!"

It is a shame some people still feel this way and have not taken the trouble to distinguish between good and bad, black or white. Maybe they have no idea that there is a difference, that could be the answer I suppose. A genuine medium wants nothing but good for everyone.

WENDY'S BELL.

I was sitting in the shop chatting with Tom who called in whenever he was in the area, and I was shocked to see that it was getting on for four o'clock and I had told my daughter that I would return to London when the sun went down. Nina, whom I had seen before, came in and asked if she could have a reading. I told her

"No, I'm sorry, I have told my daughter I will go back to London when the sun goes down, so I'm afraid there is not time to see you today. I was just telling Tom I have a lot of letters to catch up with before I go, but please sit for a while if you like while I get on with them. Tom will keep you company."

Tom and she sat and chattered while I sorted out what I had to do.

From time to time, as I was writing, I could see out of the corner of my mind's eye a small silver bell on the end of what looked like a wand. I dismissed it, as I did not understand what it meant, but it kept returning, making a merry tinkling sound. "Tinkle, tinkle, tinkle," every few seconds. It was not ringing, as an ordinary bell would do. It tinkled, literally "tinkled."

At four thirty the telephone rang; it was my daughter; her first words were,

"What are you doing? Why are you still there? The sun has gone down. You should be on your way back to London."

"Oh don't worry my love, I am catching the next train at five o clock. I will be there by 6.30 p.m."

The little bell then created an urgent, agitated tinkling and Nina began to cry. Pleading with me she said,

"Oh please Selena, please don't go. I really do need a reading. Please stay and see me."

Nessa was still talking to me on the telephone so I said,

"OK, Nina you win" Then to Nessa, "I will catch the 6 o clock train. I must give this lady a reading. I'll be in London at 7.30 p.m."

"All right, but be sure you don't miss that train." Said Nessa.

I promised I would definitely be on the 6-o clock train and sent Tom away. Nina and I went into the consulting room. In her reading, Nina was told what to do about her flat (which she had been very concerned about) and that help was on the way so that she could get the repairs that were urgent done. A large house was seen standing in what was described as 'a riot of colour.'

"You will go to this house and take care of someone there when the garden is a riot of colour. There are also some children there who need you."

The children and their father were talked about at some length and Nina was left in no doubt who this family were or where the house was situated. All this time, for about half an hour, the little wand with its bell kept making me aware of its presence. I said to Nina

"Please give me a minute - something is going on I don't understand. I am sorry but I must sort this out. There is little bell which 'tinkles' and it seems to be on the end of a wand."

I went on, "It sounds ridiculous, I know, but it reminds me, I don't know why, of Peter Pan and Tinkerbell. Peter Pan keeps coming into my head and I'm sure this little bell has something to do with Peter Pan, but what?"

Nina gasped, and burst into tears. Through her tears she said,

"Oh, I know what it means. How wonderful! How wonderful! You have answered my questions and given me proof of life after death. Thank you Selena."

I took her in my arms, waited for her to calm down and then said to her

"Well, I don't understand what it's all about. What has Peter Pan and Tinkerbell to do with life after death?"

"Oh Selena." My client said. "I will explain. The house you have told me about in such detail belongs to my sister and her husband. The garden is always very colourful but it is a riot of colour in the late autumn. My sister made it so. She also built up a small nursery and many people come from all over the country to visit it and buy plants."

"But just a minute", I said. "You are being told that, after the flat you are living in now has been sorted out, you must go there in the autumn and keep up the good work. Take over and keep it going; it must not be left to nature's whim after all the work your sister has put into it."

"But I don't know anything about gardening. Every plant looks the same to me, and I don't get on very well with my brother-in-law, but if she wants me to go I will. If what you say about my flat is right, then the times will coincide nicely."

"Don't worry, your sister's hand will guide yours. She will show you what to do and how to do it. But what has all this to do with Peter Pan and Tinkerbell?"

Nina explained, "When my mother was pregnant with my sister she loved to be read to. My father sat by her side and read Peter Pan to her every night. When my sister was born she was called Wendy, after the girl in the story. Wendy died on Wednesday, which is why I am here today and why I needed a reading so very much." We finished the reading after Wendy had reassured Nina that she was happy and that the relationship between Nina and her brother-in-law would be much improved.

We both went joyfully home. My faith had been restored yet again, and by a tiny thing like a bell on the end of a wand.

MEETING THE STARS.

I was asked to give my services at a charity bazaar organised by the 'Young Variety Club', and I saw a number of well-known actors and actresses, most of whom came to see me later for a proper reading.

The charity charged them £5 each. We were only given 10-15 minutes for each person at the function, as the organisers wanted to make as much money as possible for charity. There is not much I can do in fifteen minutes. So I gave them all one of my cards and suggested that they could have a longer reading with me privately if they wished.

One of those who came to see me later was an up-and-coming young actor Michael Pread. He was hoping to be called to rehearse for a show called 'Abracadabra' at the Lyric Hammersmith.

He was told "You will be called for the Lyric and Abracadabra will be great fun to do.

Later you will be offered something which, I assure you, will be very successful. You will be very hesitant at first about taking the part, as you'll be asked to dress in green."

"I HATE green." Michael said vehemently.

"Yes I know, you hate green, but you will wear it, you will wear green from head to toe. The play will have something to do with Sherwood. I don't know if this is the name of the person who'll offer you the part, or if it is the name of the show, but Sherwood is written here in large letters.

Do not let the opportunity pass you by. Take it, even if you do have doubts about being dressed in green."

He was also told that his wedding would cost a million pounds. His friend who had come with him had a good laugh about this, saying

"He doesn't have a million pennies, so how can he have a wedding costing a million pounds?"

After the show 'Abracadabra' closed Michael did get the part described in his reading. He was given the wonderful part of Robin Hood in a television production, and has since had his million pound wedding on television in the 'soap' drama Dallas. He was cast as the Prince of Moravia and married one of the heroines of that 'soap.' They said it cost a million pounds to stage the lavish wedding.

In the book in which clients write their comments on the readings he wrote,

"Truth is beauty - beauty truth, that's all you know, and all you need to know on earth." Keats wrote something like that but he said it better - MP 28th November 1983."

TESTIMONIALS.

The book in which Michael wrote his comments is not kept for clients to praise me, but to prove the truth of what was said. They are asked to write their comments and to say if what they heard was truth. Or, if what they were told meant nothing to them, to write that just as clearly. Another comment in my book reads,

"I had a sitting at Eastbourne with Madam Selena last July and was truly amazed at what she told me, as she spoke about things only I knew, and pin-pointed a traumatic time in great detail fifteen years ago in my life. It was incredible. She was in trance at the time and my mother gave me a message through her, the details of which showed me that my mother knew what was happening to me. She also related how she, my Mother, had passed over. Madam Selena could have known nothing of this, which happened twenty years ago. While waiting to see Madam Selena, I met a man who said she would tell me things from way back and that I would be amazed at what she knew. This I was." Elizabeth Bridge.

PROOF FOR THE SCEPTICS

Many people come in saying "I don't believe in this sort of thing, but my wife (husband, friend,) made me come." My book is full of comments like,

"I was a disbeliever, but after this reading I am totally convinced that there is such a thing as survival after death."

I am not praising myself when I say this, as whatever happens has very little to do with me. I just have to be there. The rest is up to Spirit, or whoever is in charge. Before I start a reading, I say my prayer, and ask that the person who is sitting with me is given the truth, that they have the answers they need rather than those they want, and Thy will, not mine, be done. And then whatever 'happens', happens. I always give the client a tape recording of the reading because no one remembers what has been said. They only remember what they wanted to hear, and that is recalled in their own words, so they can easily make it fit what they like. If they do not hear what they wanted to hear, then they very seldom remember anything at all, until what was said in the reading is happening, and then they try and search their memory.

"What did she say about that? She talked about that, you know. What did she tell me, what was it?"

This is where the fitting in begins. Some mediums rely on this, as it ensures that the person will return for another reading. I feel that too frequent readings are a waste of the client's time and money. And they take my time from someone else who could benefit. I will not see clients too often, say, more than once a year. A reading should enable them to get on with their own lives, NOT be relied on to resolve every problem that crops up. Everyone is responsible for his, or her, own lives and decisions; a reading is meant to help clarify things for the client, not to make decisions for them. That is their responsibility. A great many people come away from other medium's readings and say,

"Guess what, she/he said this, or that, or the other."

Whereas, in fact, she/he did not say that, - THEY did, and the medium picked up on what they said and elaborated on it. When a client has a tape recording of the reading they cannot possibly say that or make things fit. Each word is chosen with great care to mean one thing and one thing only. They may try and make it fit, but when what was spoken about is happening; there is no doubt about what is meant. I never ask my clients "What do you want from this reading?" even when 'The Management' seem to offer no help. This happens sometimes when the timing is not right, or when something else has to happen before the client can be advised. At such times I have to tell them

"There is nothing I can do here today. I am sorry. Please come another time and we'll try again."

The first time this happened was a very salutary lesson for me. I was still in Eastbourne and had been working very hard. When I work for long periods without a break the readings are usually very good, the power builds up, and everything flows smoothly. I called my next client in feeling quite confident.

We sat for a reading and my client was informed that her daughter was in Australia but that something had happened to make my client feel distressed, almost destroyed.

I also knew that these feelings had something to do with her daughter's behaviour, but more than that I did not know. I said to her,

"There is nothing more I can say my darling, I'm sorry."

"Then I will come back again. I know you are the one to give me my answers." she replied.

"But I can't tell you any thing if I am not being given any help. I don't see how you can be told anything another time, if they won't tell us now."

"But I know you are the one to tell me. I shall come back on Friday at 11.00 a.m."

So saying she got up said goodbye and left, leaving me in a state of shock. Why was there nothing to tell her? I did not understand. Today was Wednesday. She had come from Hunstanton in Norfolk, especially to see me. Her friend had been for a reading the previous week, and had been given so much proof of survival that the tape had been played over and over again, and she had telephoned all her friends and told them about it.

My client said she would stay with this friend until Friday. I 'died' a thousand deaths between that Wednesday afternoon and the Friday morning, terrified that I would have nothing to tell her. She arrived on the Friday morning at exactly eleven o'clock. I put the reading off as long as I could by chattering about anything I could think of, and finally decided that I was being very silly. My client had come for a reading and I really must get on with it. I said my prayer, and the reading flowed as though a tap had been turned on. Many intimate details concerning her daughter and herself were talked about and explanations given. She was also told that her daughter would come home at Christmas, bringing with her a young man, whom she would want to marry. The reading lasted an hour and a half - so much needed to be explained and understood.

After the reading, when my client told me what had been said, I was mystified, and shaking my head I said,

"Well, I don't understand, if you could be told so much today, I don't see why you couldn't have been told on Wednesday. Why is it all right for you to be told now and not then, I wonder?"

"Oh, I understand completely." she said.

"Well then I wish you would tell me."

"My friend and I had a visitor yesterday, a priest, and he explained a great many things about gay people. How some people go through these phases and come out the other side, whilst others decide they are better individuals and happier living with someone of the same sex. If you had told me the details of my daughter's life at present, and all the other things you have told me today, before I'd had my talk with the priest, I would probably have killed you in anger, and certainly would not have understood. As it is, I can accept everything you have said because it explains so many things."

She went on to say "Before my daughter joined the Nursing Corps we were so close - we were more like sisters than mother and daughter, we told each other everything, nothing was taboo. Then she, my daughter, was posted to Australia and I didn't see her for months. She came home on leave during the summer and we were like two complete strangers. I asked her what she had been doing and who her friends were, as I had always done, and she shut me out. She refused to answer any of my questions, getting very angry with me every time I mentioned Australia; it was terrible - we had nothing in common any more. She was like a stranger, I felt shunned and totally alone, more alone than I had been when she was away. Do you know what I mean? When she returned to Australia I felt that I no longer knew this person - I couldn't understand what had happened to change things so drastically, now I know and it is such a relief!"

In the reading she had been told that her daughter had formed a relationship with another girl in Australia and had found it impossible to talk to her mother about it. She felt guilty, and so felt she had to shut her mother out.

Now the mother understood and was laughing and crying with relief. Up until then, she had not been able to understand her daughter's behaviour, and had been blaming herself.

I had a letter from her the following Christmas, to say that her daughter had brought a young man home and that they were to be married very soon.

I had learned another valuable lesson. WHEN the time is right, we will be shown. Not until then.

If ever I find there are no answers now, I do not blame 'The Management,' or myself, I simply say,

"We must try another time."

Some people find this very hard to accept. They become concerned and think that I won't tell them because I can see something dreadful that is going to happen to them.

It takes a lot of careful explanation to convince them that this is not so. I usually end up by telling them the story of the lady from Hunstanton.

VOICES OTHER THAN MINE ON THE TAPES

I find great difficulty in asking people for money, and I decided that I should get someone to run the shop for me. I had put a notice on my waiting room door saying that I needed someone to make appointments, take payments for readings, and sell my paintings.

Three girls came in and asked about it. We talked for an hour or so, and I then gave them each one of my cards. I asked them to ring me later, when I would tell them what I had decided. The youngest one showed great interest in the job. She telephoned the next day, and said,

"I really do want to come and work with you. When can I come?"

"Come tomorrow. Why don't you come tomorrow? That would be fine," I said,

I had already been 'shown' that she would not come. But I knew it was necessary to keep the contact going; no one ever steps over the threshold of my room for no reason.

She did not come, neither did she bother to telephone, but the oldest one, Monica, did telephone a week later to make an appointment for a reading for herself and her daughter, Tracy. They came the following week.

Both of them were overjoyed with their readings, and went away happily three hours later. The next morning, Monica telephoned and asked,

"Are there usually Spirit voices on the tapes?"

"Oh, um, I don't know, sometimes people say there are. Why?" I asked.

"We played the tapes last night and again this morning and there are voices other than yours and ours." Monica said, she was quite excited by this time.

I tried to calm her down and asked her "Are you sure there are OTHER voices, my voice sounds quite different sometimes during readings."

"Yes, we are sure, the voices are there while you are speaking." Monica said.

They brought the tapes in a few days later and asked me to listen to them.

As I have already mentioned, I do not like listening to tapes of my readings, but they were so excited that I agreed to do so.

There certainly were other voices on the tapes. There were odd words agreeing with what was being said and longer sentences saying something like

"This is for the book."

Monica's nickname was also called out by one of the voices. There is certainly no way that I could have known her nickname or anything else about her life.

Monica was so impressed with it all; she took on the job of making my appointments, which she did very well. She made me work.

I always made appointments from the evening backwards through the day, putting things off for as long as possible. Monica started by making the first one at ten a.m. each day.

As she had had a reading herself, she knew how people felt when they came out from a reading, and she invited them to sit in the waiting room for a while before going out into the big noisy world again.

Most people are a bit disorientated when they come out from my rooms and it is always better if they can sit and 'come back to earth' before the outside world hits them with its noise and frustration.

A few weeks after she had started working for me, some girls were sitting in the waiting room with Monica talking about the readings they had just had, when one said

"How did she know? How did she know so many things about such a complicated situation?"

One of the others said, laughingly, "God's coming for a reading next week. Don't worry, she'll know just who he is."

Monica was still chuckling to herself when I came out with my client and said to me

"I really don't know why you are always so worried about doing readings, you must know that what is said is always right."

I did, I do, but I always prefer to sit in the waiting room and let whatever goes on in the consulting room, go on without me.

I never feel worthy of being in there. Once I'm in there and working, it is all right. I can stay there all day and all night seeing one after another.

The longer I work the better it seems to be. I suppose it's because the power in the room builds up. I am recharged every time I do a reading; no matter how tired I am before I start, it never interferes with what happens, and neither do I need to eat, drink or prove my mortality by going to the loo. The time passes without my being aware of it.

I have found that it is better not to have any time in between clients. Breaking off to eat or chatter seems to break the flow.

READING FOR A COACH PARTY.

I saw twenty people one Whit Sunday. As one left, another came in. I was astounded to find that it was dark when I came out with the last one. There is no window in my room so unless someone mentions it, I have no idea of time. I had worked straight through from 9.00 a.m. until 11.30 p.m. no breaks for a cup of tea, or anything else - and I felt great.

When I left my rooms to go home, most of that day's clients were standing there together, chattering and laughing. I was so astounded to see them all together I went over to talk to them and find out what they were all doing there!

One of them broke away from the others and told me that they had hired a coach especially to come and see me.

They came from the Tunbridge Wells, Sevenoaks area. They had heard so much about my readings from friends and neighbours, all of whom had had sittings with me over the years, and who'd had proof that what had been said had come to pass. They decided to club together and come to see me en-masse.

Now they were all waiting for the coach driver to come and escort them to the coach for the journey home.

GUIDANCE STRAIGHT FROM THE HORSE'S MOUTH.

One of my clients transcribed some of the tape recording of her reading for me. My client had been inquiring why mediumship seems so easy for some people whilst others who desperately want to be of service to their fellow human beings, can not develop any of the gifts of the Spirit.

Some of what was said is shared with us on the following pages.

"Just as there are many people on earth looking for trouble to cause, and mischief to get up to, so there are in Spirit.

Death does not produce instant wisdom. Time and experience are just as necessary there as they are on earth. It is wrong to think that every Spirit can, or will, communicate through a medium.

In Spirit, will and desire, still play a big part. If, when a person was on earth, they had strong feelings about intruding on other people's privacy, so it will be still in Spirit. They will still find it difficult to intrude, unless something justifies such an intrusion.

The great thing about mediumship is that it is a natural faculty. So many people think it can be handed to them like a meal on a plate, and all they have to do is go to mediumship development classes. They want to develop, cannot do so, and get resentful when they see others that can.

Most of us possess mediumship as children, but as we grow up we get so bogged down with material things and intellectualism, that we shut it out by arguing with ourselves and questioning, and so close the top of our head to the answers.

It comes as a great surprise to many people that there are some very good mediums who are totally irreligious.

All mediumship means is that we obtain the help of one or more wise spirits, who help us to unfold latent powers.

But if the natural faculty is not there, nothing can provide it."

ONE SMALL WORD PROVES SURVIVAL

My lady from Wales was smiling happily at the end of her reading.

Her husband had proved he was there, without a doubt. During the reading many things had been spoken about, things that only he could have ever known. But she had asked for one word that would prove beyond a doubt that it was her husband who was communicating.

I asked for that proof. It is always very difficult for me if I know there is one specific thing the client wants. I worry that I will not get it right and that puts up barriers because it has now become an ego thing; and I feel I must do it!

She was told, "He can be much more help to you from there than he could possibly be from here."

No response from my lady.

Then, apparently, after I had argued with someone unseen by my client for a few minutes, I then turned back to her and said,

"I am sorry darling, I was wrong. Your husband says, "I can be more 'USE' to you now from where I am, than I could possibly be when I was there with you."

"That proves it, that's my husband!"

"How can you know that now, and not before?" I asked, "What difference is there between those two statements?"

"The fact that you said the word 'use'. That one word 'use." she said.

I asked her "How can one word make so much difference?" and was told,

"All the difference in the world, my dear. When my husband was here, he was totally disabled and said to me every day of his life "Darling, I am no use to you." Before he died he said to me, "IF there is anything after this life, I will come back and tell you, and, try and be of some use to you." So you see that one word means the difference between survival and nothing to me."

I felt quite chastened by that experience, and vowed I would listen more carefully in future.

"DO YOU TELL EVERYONE THE SAME THING?"

After a reading everyone says how tired I look. This lasts for a few minutes and then I am back again and recharged. I look tired, but that's only because I'm not back from wherever it is I go. It is like coming out of meditation or waking up; it takes a little time.

If there are people around me who are shouting, it really hurts my head. Just as sitting in a car with the radio on, hurts my head. It's not the noise that hurts; it's the vibration. But noise too can be destructive. That's why so many of us are suffering these days. We are surrounded by noise. Nearly every shop or restaurant has a radio or tapes pouring out loud, crashing sounds and most of it is such a din that it cannot possibly be called music.

The streets are so noisy we cannot hear ourselves think. Mothers walk, cigarettes hanging from the mouth, with babies crying, radios playing on the buggy handle, and then they wonder why they are tired. If only they would stop, turn the radio off, talk to the child and take the trouble to find out what's wrong, they would find that they are not tired at all.

Work doesn't exhaust people. It's noise, constant noise.

We also need to guard against emotional disturbances. Such disturbances can only happen, of course, when we allow the ego to become dominant. When we want recognition, or praise for ourselves.

I did just that earlier this year. (Got myself into an emotional state, and allowed the ego to raise its ugly head.)

A Mr. Bell came for a reading. This is his account of that reading told to me by him.

"My wife, who had died earlier that year, came through and told me of the photographs I had been sorting out. They were described in detail. I was asked to change some round as I had put a great many of them on the walls of the sitting room and the bedroom, and my wife wanted different ones put up. She asked me not to make the flat a shrine to her memory, just to have one or two photographs around if I felt I still needed them, but not to cover the walls as I had been doing."

He also told me that his wife's arm and head had been damaged at birth, and all through her life she had kept her arm covered with a shawl, or something similar.

During the reading he noticed that my arm had been covered with my cape for most of the reading. (Not a thing I would normally do. Cover my arm.)

My head had shown the same marks that had bothered his wife when she was alive, marks made by forceps at birth.

He was told of a health condition in him and what to do about it -

"You must get something done about it now by natural remedies, not drugs, ask Selena for some herbs after this consultation, she will know what you need."

Towards the end of the reading, the cape was thrown off to show that the arm was fully restored, and he was asked to look at my head.

That was now back to its normal shape, she then informed him that hers was now perfectly formed as well.

He was also told "You must do something before the end of the summer to stop the water coming under the front door. Each year you mean to do it, and you always leave it until its too late, and each winter the water comes in again!"

He confirmed that everything he had been told was absolutely correct, but he found it difficult to understand how a complete stranger could know so much about his life.

After his reading he went off shaking his head in wonder. I watched him as he walked away with brisk steps looking back every few yards as though still unable to take it all in.

He telephoned two months later, asking if he could come again.

I did not feel he should need a reading again so soon, and told him so. He insisted so we made an appointment for the next week. When he arrived, I sat with him in the waiting room. I did not know what I was waiting for, but I knew I could not start a reading yet. He told me that a friend of his wife had listened to the tape and said

"That's Louise's voice. That's Louise. Oh how wonderful! How lucky you are to have been told all these things. How could a complete stranger know so much, and speak in her voice?"

He went on to tell me all that had been said and done during his reading, he told me how much happier he was now, and that his health had improved since taking the herbs he had been prescribed.

He then asked, "Did you see my Louise when you gave me my reading?"

I said "I'm sorry darling, I don't know, I never remember what has been said or what happens. It's not for me to remember, it's for you; that is why you have the tape."

"What do you mean, you don't know?" he said, "You must know, you said those things. You said she was there, and told me what she was saying."

I tried to explain but he did not understand.

He then said, "Do you tell everyone the same thing? Do you have a set patter that you give to everyone who comes?"

I could not believe my ears. For a while, I could say nothing and then, I am totally ashamed to say, I got very angry with him.

I told him to get out, saying to him "How dare you say that. After all the proof you were given. You told me a little while ago, how so many things were said that only Louise could have known - photographs described in minute details, disfigurations shown, and her friend recognising Louise's voice, the water under the door. How can you say, do I tell everyone the same thing?"

I felt that if he had cut my throat he would have hurt me less. I threw him out, and I cried and cried, saying to a friend who had come in to see me,

"What do they want, just what do they want? I give them my time, my life, every minute of every day. Do they want my blood as well?"

It was a childish self-indulgent display of the ego coming up, a totally stupid thing to do - not only or me but for him as well. I spent the rest of the day getting myself back together again, and have not knowingly seen him since. Nor have I allowed myself to get into such a state again.

During a reading, many details had been given of a life spent together with my lady client, but my client told me later that I had felt I would like to have some more definite identification. And I had asked for a name.

"How about a name, can we know your name please Sir?"

I was told. "No, we will not give you a name, we will give you a riddle. The riddle is a poem by Rabbie Burns, a tam-o-shanter, and rolling about the floor with laughter."

This had meant nothing to me, but my client laughed and said "Oh yes, yes that's my husband. You see I am Scottish, my husband was English. Rabbie Burns wrote a poem called 'Donald, where's your troosers?' My husband's name was Donald and he used to recite that poem in a terrible Scottish accent wearing a tam-o-shanter and we would roll about the floor with laughter."

She went off clutching her tape, tears of happiness rolling down her cheeks.

SHADES OF MURDER

In October 1981, Jane and Peter* came from East Anglia to see me.

They were going to Majorca on holiday the next day and wanted to spend the night in my flat, as it was easier to get to the airport from there.

I had known Peter for a number of years, but this was the first time I had met Jane and found her very attractive and sensitive. They seemed made for each other, but there was something not quite right.

I felt an edginess but could not put my finger on it. She wanted a reading before she went on her holiday.

We sat and she was told that her mother would be moving soon and where she would go.

Her children from a previous marriage and various other events that were happening in her life were spoken about, and she was shown how to cope with emotional disturbances caused by others.

Jane was then asked about a professional man.

"Is there a professional man in your family?"

"Yes, there is."

"Is he thinking of retiring?"

"No, I don't think so, why?"

A large black topped desk was seen empty. Then she was told that there would be a great deal of trouble concerning this man.

"There will be much trouble for many people and great unhappiness. Many lives will be changed by circumstances surrounding this man."

Jane had been married to the professional man spoken about, but it had not worked out and they had been divorced.

Our reading was interrupted and we agreed to continue the following morning before Jane and Peter left for their holiday, but we did not get around to it.

We all got up very late, and there was a in a great rush to get to the airport in time. Jane left her tape behind in my flat. Peter and Jane went off on their holiday. They married later that year.

Her children spend some time with them in Peter's house and the rest of the time with their father, the professional man. Jane has continued to work for this man. Peter also works as a chauffeur for him sometimes as he was banned from driving and still needs to make calls on people.

At the time of our reading, he, the professional man, was married to someone who had disappeared and who was later found murdered.

He was questioned at length by the police but was never charged and he has since married again.

*The names have been changed to protect my client.

SOME TIME FOR ME? NO.

I attended a meditation course and was enjoying the very pleasant company, and the teachings. The course was run by an old friend of mine, John. The place we were staying in had been a monastery, is still lived in by monks, and has a wonderful spiritual atmosphere, which was very conducive to what we were learning.

It is a moated castle, and a river runs close by. Swans glide by on this river, and in the moat, looking quite peaceful and beautiful, they quite often come up on to the wide sloping grass banks, if one gets too close they are very quick to attack, as I found to my cost later.

All went well until the Saturday afternoon.

It was a wonderfully sunny day, and I 'knew' that I did not want to go in for the afternoon session. I thought I just wanted to enjoy the sunshine and sit by the river. I needed to be still and quiet.

John and I had walked by the river after lunch and I had said I did not want to be indoors that afternoon and miss the sunshine.

When I am working I spend most of my time sitting in a room with no window, and I hated to miss this chance to be outside in the sun.

I had agreed to go on the weekend course because John had told me

"You must come. It will be a chance for you to relax and do what you want to do. You don't have to take part if you don't want to."

So on this afternoon I took him at his word and did what I wanted to do! At least, that is what I thought I was doing!

That evening, as I walked into the dining room for supper, John shouted at me, in front of everyone, monks and fellow students. He was telling me how unsociable, bad mannered and unhelpful I had been by not supporting him in the meeting that afternoon.

There were some very inattentive people on this course and until this day I had sat at the back of the room which meant that they found it quite difficult to play around, or slip out.

His work had been made that much more difficult because I had been missing. I learned later that John had the strange idea that I was jealous of another lady on the course who was the only one recognised by the movement as a healer. He accused me of this because I had been singing the popular song 'Jealousy' since I had come in from my afternoon in the sun.

I didn't know why I was singing that song. It reminded me of my daughter Michelle. She had sent me the words to it when she was in France studying ballet. When I had spoken with her the week before, she had said that she would be going to France for this weekend, and now I was concerned that something might have happened to her. Putting two and two together and making fifteen again!

John thought I was using this as an excuse for what he called my unreasonable behaviour.'

He felt that I had been rude to 'the healer'. I certainly had not meant to be, as I have great respect and admiration for this lady.

I often appear to be rude. I have inherited a very sharp tongue from my father, and this, coupled with the need I have to tell the truth, makes me very difficult to cope with sometimes, I am sure.

But I am equally sure I would never do, or say, anything intentionally, to hurt this person or anyone else in the movement.

I was certain that 'something' had happened 'somewhere' and my thoughts kept returning to Michelle and France.

We had no radio or newspapers in the castle, so I had to wait until the end of the course on Sunday evening to find out what was wrong and where. I asked the man who was driving John and myself back to London on Sunday evening. "Have you heard any news bulletins today?"

"No," he replied, "but it is almost six o clock, we can put the radio on for the news if you like."

We listened to the news; there was no mention of anything happening in France. John was looking satisfied, obviously thinking that he had been right all along. Then, at the end of the broadcast, the news reader spoke about a coach crash that had happened in France involving many young people.

The coach had crashed on Saturday at the same time that I had felt the overpowering need to sit in the sun and be still. John turned to me took my hand, and said,

"Sorry love. We'll get a paper when we get into London." True to his word, he asked the driver to stop at the first newsagents we found open, and he bought a paper back to the car.

We learned that many young people had indeed lost their lives, and many more were injured.

When we got to John's home, I very quickly ascertained that Michelle was not amongst them. She had changed her mind about going to France, and had stayed at home.

My being made to think about that song and Michelle had been solely to direct my feelings and thoughts to France.

Being still and quiet meant I could be of some help to those who had been killed. Help them to understand what had happened to them - not in a physical way, but mentally and spiritually.

This is why I had needed to stay quietly outside in the sun and allow my Spirit to roam freely.

Not be shut-up inside with a lot of people discussing the finer points of meditation!

HOW IMPORTANT IS OUR NAME?

Shanee and Clive had invited me to spend the evening with them, after my treatment from Shanee, who is a natural healer, although she was not aware of it at the time.

She only knew that she wanted to lay hands on people. She had given herself some credibility by becoming a qualified chiropractor and an acupuncturist.

A great many people do this, not knowing they are healers. They train as nurses, doctors, or in one or other of the healing professions and so unknowingly use their gifts for the benefit of others.

Shanee had been named Gudrun by her mother and called by that name all her life until she went to America. While there she met some American Indians and stayed with them learning their ways.

The chief called her to him and told her "You have the wrong name, you have been given your sister's name."

"No, I don't have a sister."

"Ah, but you did have a sister who died, and who had been called Gudrun. When you were born your mother gave you her name. This means that you are living your sister's Karma as well as yours, that's why your life has been so difficult."

Shanee had not known about her sister and found this difficult to believe, but he insisted that it was so and continued.

"I hereby give you a new name, from now on your name is Shanee."

Shanee liked the name and decided to use it from then. Her life changed course, and from that day good things started happening for her.

She also found that the Red Indian had been quite right about the name Gudrun. Her mother had lost a child of a few months while fleeing from the Russians in Czechoslovakia and when she had a second daughter she'd given her the first child's name.

It was soon after returning to England with her new name that Shanee met Clive.

Clive is also a qualified acupuncturist. He had been working with the Social Services, helping to run a hostel for teenage girls in the care of the Local Authority, in order to pay for his training.

They lived in Hackney. There had been a lot of trouble at the hostel, and it had attracted a bad press. Clive had tried to put things right, but was fighting a losing battle.

We were talking after supper, and Clive said

"I don't know what I'm to do now, the hostel is sure to be closed after all this trouble and I really need a job to enable me to complete my training."

I heard a voice say,

"He will be a Spiritual hairdresser."

"A what?" I exclaimed.

Clive repeated what he had been saying, thinking I was talking to him.

"No, not you Clive", I said. "I'm sorry, did you say a Spiritual Hairdresser?" I asked, directing my gaze to where the voice had come from. Clive and Shanee were looking rather shocked at my talking to myself. I asked them if they would mind waiting a minute, as I must get this sorted out.

I was aware of a strong, beautiful being, fair and luminous, who radiated strength and compassion.

He smiled and assured me, "Yes, I did say a spiritual hairdresser-" He explained, "There are many acupuncture points on the head, and if the hair is not hanging correctly on these points, the whole being is 'out of tune'.

Take these examples; if someone ruffles the hair on your head. If the wind blows it a different way from the way you usually wear it. Or your hairdresser persuades you to try a new hairstyle, it doesn't matter that everyone else says 'Oh, that looks good,' or something similar, if the hair is not lying correctly on the acupuncture points, you will not feel right.

"It's just not me" I hear you say, and other people's comments make no difference to the way you feel. You will want to rush straight home and brush it out until it is as you feel it should be.

Then, and only then, will you feel right, and the feeling of discomfort or unease will disappear."

I said "Oh, I see, yes, I have felt like that sometimes."

He went on "Your hair is your social antennae. If it is necessary for you to be emotionally involved with people 'en masse' then you will allow your hair to grow and flow. If you feel the need to be efficient and uninvolved emotionally, you will cut the hair short or tie it back. The Army insists on short hair because when a man is involved in a war he is fighting for his own, and his comrade's survival. Sometimes he is called upon to kill fellow human beings, and that needs self-discipline and non-involvement with the emotions. This is also why the Police are not as efficient as they were.

The authorities no longer insist on policemen's hair being cut short. . It can, and often does, hang over the collar. If you look at these men with their hair hanging down their neck, you will surely see that the shoes are also unkempt! I tell you this makes these men more vulnerable to what is happening around them. Instead of standing back and assessing the situation, the emotions come to the fore and they rush in.

Remember the time you called 'the Sixties'. All the young people were talking about love and togetherness. How was their hair? Yes, it was long and flowing. Now we have gone a full circle and the young ones today are shaving their heads. They no longer want to be sharing, loving beings. They wish to look out for themselves with little or no thought for others."

I asked "What about monks; they shave their heads?"

"Yes, my child, but they are in enclosed Orders. They are not out in the world. They must be insular to be able to devote their thoughts and energies to prayer."

He then bade us farewell, and said that he would come again. We sat for the next hour or so discussing what had been said. Clive said he had always felt he wanted to cut hair and in actual fact had been cutting Shanee's hair for the previous few months!

I went home still thinking about what had been said, and marvelling at the ways Spirit finds to tell us things.

A number of friends and patients found themselves at the mercy of Clive's scissors over the next few weeks and they all said how different they felt; they felt 'right' now.

Soon after this, Clive and Shanee came to my house for a reading.

As soon as we sat down the same being appeared, looking even brighter than before, shining with a golden glow round his form.

Clive was told that he and this being had been together in previous lives and that they had chosen to work together in this incarnation of Clive's to be of help to mentally handicapped people.

Clive had certainly found he was always being put in the path of those in need of healing in this way.

The 'being' reminded Clive that in one of his previous lives he had been very cruel to anyone whom he considered to be 'slow of mind'.

He went on to say

"You have done so well and helped so many beyond the call of duty in this life you have completed that part of your Karma. You have speeded things up by giving so much, and now the rest of your life is for you. No longer do you have to be surrounded by those affected by mental illness. From now on, the people around you will be positive and outgoing. You will work for yourself."

Clive and Shanee completed their training, and are now running their own practice and have a lovely house in Wales, this house was described to them in detail in another reading.

For the last part of his training as an acupuncturist Clive needed someone to be his 'patient.'

As I had been having treatment from Shanee, he asked me if I would go to Leamington Spa, where he was completing his training, each Friday and have acupuncture to balance up my energy flow which, he said, was unbalanced.

Both he and Shanee considered this would be good for me as it would put my physical body right. I had reservations about this as I knew my energies had been changed spiritually to allow me to be used for my work, but I agreed to do it with some trepidation.

It meant catching the train from Paddington at 6.40 a.m. each Friday but I did not mind that. I love the early mornings, and long train journeys.

On the first Friday, Clive was writing his report on my pulses and general appearance. I was lying on the couch.

In my mind I 'saw' myself lying on a couch in a room similar to the one we were in. This couch, (the one in my vision,) was on the other side of the room and the walls were pink, - not the colour of the room we were in, which was a pale cream. .

I watched this scene fascinated. As I watched, I saw Clive and another man talking animatedly, and I noticed that there were a number of other people standing in the doorway looking very anxious.

On top of me, covering my left side, with its head on my shoulder, was a large, green dragon. It was very beautiful, but it was crying bitter tears - and I was saying to the ones huddled round the door,

"I told you this would happen - I told you. Why didn't you listen?"

I told Clive what I had seen; he seemed rather bemused and did not know what to make of it. I asked him what a green dragon stood for in Chinese acupuncture and he told me it represented the life force.

Some time after this, the man who was Clive's tutor came in and I was perturbed to see that this was the man I had seen in my vision talking animatedly with Clive.

I told this man of my apprehension, and that I felt sure that if my energies were changed I would die because I was not here for me; I was here for others. If the energies were altered so that I could no longer work with Spirit, then there would be no reason for me to be here.

The tutor, Clive and I talked about this for some time and they both agreed that I might well lose the ability to work with Spirit if the energies were made to flow as they 'should' normally; but, I would be much fitter and that to them was more important. Clive's tutor said,

"Our job is to heal the whole being not a part of the person. We do not say we will, or can, help to strengthen any single limb or organ; we heal the whole person and if that means losing your ability to be used by Spirit, so be it."

I went to Leamington Spa each Friday for five weeks, and each week became more and more sick, - my right leg and hip were so painful I could hardly walk.

I developed a dreadful cough and became weaker as each week passed. I was assured that this was all right.

"Often acupuncture accentuates weakness before healing takes place." I was told.

I continued to have my doubts that I was doing the right thing. During this time I did no work, saw no clients and put my general weakness down to the fact that I was not working.

As long as I see clients for readings or healing, I am fit, and recharged with each one. I always become sick if I stop seeing clients. Both Clive and his tutor began to get cross with me for my apparent ingratitude.

"You are always complaining about some aspect of the treatment, always asking questions." "Why does this happen?" "Why did I have that reaction?" " Why can't you just accept that we know what we are doing and not ask so many questions?"

On my last visit to the clinic, I had an uncontrollable bout of coughing and was hanging over the side of the couch trying to stop coughing and get my breath. Clive was banging my back and trying hard to comfort me.

This was the scene, which confronted Mr Worsley; the Head of the College, as he, with half a dozen other tutors and students marched into the room. I turned to meet his gaze, scarlet from the prolonged coughing.

He stood quite still; looked shocked for a second, then, shook himself and came over to the couch where I was lying. Why did he seem so shocked?

Was it my scarlet face? Or because Clive had seemed to be so intimate? - After all, he did have one arm round me. Or was it because he saw something familiar in this scene? He started his examination of my pulses telling Clive and the others with him what he thought.

He told Clive which 'points' he should activate today, turned on his heels and marched out again, students and tutors trailing behind him.

Clive asked me to sit on the edge of the couch with my back to him. He then proceeded to put the needles in the points he had been told to use - one in the top of my head, some in my back, others in the ankles.

Within seconds I could feel my life force pulling away from me. I fought to hold on to this, trying at the same time to tell Clive to get the needles out. I knew I would die if he did not do so. He tried to get me to lie down. I fought against this, knowing that if I did I would not get up again.

Clive ran out to try and find his tutor, but could not do so, as he had gone with the Head of the College and was now in another building. He eventually came back and took the needles out. By this time I was so cold he laid me on the couch and covered me with all the blankets he could find. I lay there feeling as though I was in an icy sea with waves crashing over me. I was shaking with cold - or was it fear?

It was now eleven thirty and Clive had to leave me as he had other patients to see before his afternoon training session, and I was left to get myself back together.

It was some time during the next few hours that I realised I was in the room I had seen in my 'vision' on my first morning at the college- pink walls bed facing the window. The College closed at 5.30 p.m. and someone called a taxi to take me to the station.

I left the College in the taxi and knew no more until the next day when I found myself in the front room at home.

How did I get there? I do not know; I must have caught a train from Leamington Spa to Paddington, then a bus or taxi from Paddington to my house. I have no memory of any of the journey or of the hours that had passed between leaving the College and finding myself at home the next afternoon.

Twenty-one lost hours! I was still very shaky and cold and felt as though I was in a 'zombie-like' state. Clive and Shanee came to see me the next week to see how I was, as they had been very concerned about me.

They were told, by the 'Spirit being' who had come to talk to Clive on the previous occasions.

"The sole purpose of HER going through that experience was to show you, and for you to show others at the College; that the points you used last Friday must NEVER be used by a trainee without adequate supervision because it is very dangerous."

I had gone against my intuition by agreeing to allow Clive to treat me in the first place, so Spirit decided that as I had been too stupid to listen, they may as well make some use of my stupidity - 'They,' being 'The Management' of course.

It took me about three months to get myself back to some semblance of normality.

Why, oh why, don't I listen?

Wouldn't you think I'd have learnt something by now?

OCTOBER SONG

I was back in Eastbourne and at 4.30 p.m. on a Friday afternoon in October, the telephone rang. It was Angela, a girl who had been to see me in May. She said

"May I come and see you? Please, I desperately need to see you before we go away."

"They have already closed the pier entrance gates, my love", I said, "so you can't come here. I'll come to you if you tell me where you are. But let's talk about it now and see if we can sort it out for you. What's the trouble?"

I felt that if Angela just needed someone to talk to, and it would be less expensive for her to chatter over the telephone than for me to make the journey and ask her to pay for a reading which I felt she didn't need.

She told me that her husband was a ghostwriter and needed to feel secure to be able to get on with his work, but at that time they were both feeling very insecure.

She had been to see me five months previously, and her husband, whose identity I had not known until after the reading, had been the previous month, so I did not feel that either of them should need another reading so soon.

She told me that in their readings they had both been given the description of a house, which they had been 'told' they would buy, and they would be very happy there.

October was mentioned in the readings, but apparently it was not made clear in what context.

During the summer she had been to a so-called Christian gathering - a week's Crusade where they had told her that she was putting herself and her family in danger by associating with mediums, and that she must stop, or she would be possessed by the devil.

They hounded her for days until she was too frightened to leave her house in case she bumped into any of them. (The Christians)

She had sent her daughter away to school to shield her from these people and their accusations.

They had insisted that my client must be cleansed of the devil and must give her life to Jesus. The emotional blackmail was so strong that, as the week's Crusade came to an end, she went to the front of the hall where the meeting was being held, and confessed that she had been consorting with the devil by seeing a clairvoyant.

They had taken her into a back room and subjected her to all sorts of abuse. After this, they would not leave her alone, accosting her in the streets, shops, anywhere she went, until she became so distressed that she had to have treatment from her doctor.

This was the state she was in when she telephoned me. I went to her flat that evening and let her talk it out.

Then I told her "You must leave all this abuse in the past where it belongs. While you keep going over the things that were said you are perpetuating those feelings and keeping the fear going, making yourself miserable again and again - repeating history. You must stop thinking about it, stop talking about it, and direct your mind to now and tomorrow, not back to yesterday."

We talked for a long time afterwards about many things, including this book, and she was shown how important it is to think and speak in a positive manner. She was told,

"Thoughts and words do not just disappear into the night. Whatever we are thinking or saying is exactly what we are creating for ourselves."

As Angela had told me on the telephone that afternoon that her husband was a 'ghost-writer.' I thought 'maybe that was the main reason for the contact to be made again.'

I had taken a tape recording of the first ninety minutes of these writings with me, as I was sure I was going to need a 'ghost-writer.' Is he the one?

I felt I would never be able to write a book on my own.

So many people had said I ought to write one, but I fought against it, believing that I was not capable of doing any thing of the sort, owing to my lack of formal education, a fact to which I have already referred earlier in these pages.

I cannot express myself or explain what I mean in proper English, so how could I possibly write a book? I knew nothing about punctuation, grammar or spelling, all of which are necessary when writing.

However, so many people kept telling me that I must put my experiences down on paper for others to read, that in the end I gave up protesting and sat with pen and paper, not knowing where to start.

Childhood? Now? Where?

The pen started writing at 'It was a quiet' etc. and it just went on from there, flowing as though the words could not wait to get on the paper quickly enough. When I told friends and clients what I was doing, without exception they said,

"Oh, you must put the bit in about so and so." I had forgotten about so many of the things written here until others reminded me, but, when I started to write, it all came tumbling back and was verified by the people concerned. However, I still felt that my writing would not be good enough and that I needed a 'ghost-writer.'

Whilst I was talking with my client in the kitchen, her husband agreed to listen to the tape and see if he would be interested in ghost writing for me.

My client and I joined him after we had sorted out what she had to do now.

He was still listening to the tape and when we tried to talk to him he told us to,

"Be quiet. I, want to hear what happens next."

When the tape came to an end, he said to me

"You don't need a ghost-writer you have a style of your own. Just go home and get on with your writing. No one else could do it justice, you must do it."

We all came to the conclusion that the afternoon telephone call had been necessary for all of us to benefit and benefit we had. I left them both in a much better frame of mind at 11.30 p.m. and went home to get on with this book.

They later found the house exactly as it had been described in their readings and bought it with a bridging loan from the bank which was very expensive.

But they were still unable to sell their flat and things were getting a bit desperate on the financial front!

Angela rang again a few weeks later, saying they still had not sold their flat.

"Please help, please", she pleaded.

She was told "Don't worry, someone is on the way to you and you will find a buyer quite soon."

I promised I would say my prayers about it, and so should they. A couple bought the flat the next week - so our prayers were answered.

Before they moved in, the husband visited the new house, and while tidying the garden found a piece of wood which he was about to throw on the bonfire when he saw that it was a nameplate which obviously belonged to the house. When he took a good look at it he saw that it had been fixed to a tree at some time.

After he had cleaned all the mud and leaves from it, he telephoned me excitedly saying,

"We now understand what was meant when someone spoke about 'October' in the reading all those months ago."

The old nameplate has been re-sited and proudly proclaims ''October House' to all who pass by.

HEALING AND DISAPPOINTMENT IN EASTBOURNE.

One weekend in 1982, John and I visited his mother in Eastbourne. (He of the castle course) John had told me of her suffering and I offered some of my time to see if she could be helped with healing.

When we arrived she was suffering badly, unable to speak properly or breathe easily. Her body was being eaten up with cancer. The family had lost all hope of her ever being well again.

We had a healing session in John's parents' flat that evening. As I waited, standing behind her, 1 felt the strong presence of a Red Indian girl. She had on a leather dress. There were no shoes on her feet and her hair was in plaits.

When the healing session was over and 1 was back in my own body again, John's mother sat quite still for some minutes and then she spoke. To our common astonishment, her voice was quite normal again and she said,

"I feel full of love for the whole world. I want to put right everything that I have ever done wrong. I will make it up to everyone if they will let me. I know, I will invite all the family up here tomorrow for a celebration and make it up with them."

Of course, no one other than her husband, John and I knew what had happened during that healing session, and no one was aware of the changes that had taken place in her.

By this time, it was past 10.00 p.m. and we left her to go to bed.

Before I left her I exhorted her not to start running around like a two-year-old, but to continue to take it easy. The next day she was able to walk down the three flights of stairs from her flat carrying all she needed for an afternoon on the sea front. (Something she had not been able to do for a long time)

She achieved this with no difficulty whatever; no breathlessness, no dizziness, nothing but a feeling of wellbeing and love.

During the afternoon while we were sitting on the sea front I asked her if she had any connection with Red Indians.

She replied "No, I'm sure I haven't. No I don't know of any Red Indians. Why do you ask?"

"Oh, I just wondered." I had been wondering why a Red Indian girl had come to help with her healing.

Healing is different from readings in as much as I am aware of what is happening the whole time - standing on the outside looking in as it were, and always aware of the Spirit or Spirits who are helping with the healing. I had never felt the presence of the Indian girl before.

An Indian Doctor comes to help when there are problems with the vascular system: a Nun arrives and gives her peace to those whose problems are mainly psychosomatic. There are a few others who come at different times who I recognise, but never a Red Indian girl in bare feet.

John's mother came to me later that evening and told me that she had been speaking to a relative of hers on the telephone and had been reminded that her nephew was married to a Red Indian girl!

This couple had been informed of John's mother's condition weeks before and had promised to ask for help with their prayers. The girl had also written to her people in America asking for their help. They certainly had helped.

Later that evening, John's Father opened a bottle of champagne to celebrate his wife's newly found freedom from breathlessness, bitterness and pain.

John's mother invited the rest of the family, John's brother Peter, his wife and child, (Peter ran the Hotel next door, owned by John's mother and father,) to join in the celebration.

They declined, which hurt her very much, but they were not to know of the changes that had taken place.

They knew about the healing by now because they had seen the difference in her physically, but the inner change? How could they know? How could anyone have known?

There had been a great amount of tension surrounding the family for years. It takes a long time for people to recognise a change in others, when we have always seen them behaving in one way; we continue to treat them as we have become used to doing and the chance of reconciliation goes by.

We, John, his mother and father and I, enjoyed the champagne. She wanted to throw away all her pills and potions and do a dance, she felt so wonderful.

I explained that although she felt, and was, much better, she must continue to take it easy and must not take on too much.

No shopping, or doing the washing, she must continue to leave all that to others and just enjoy feeling better.

I insisted that she must continue to follow her doctor's instructions. When he thought that she was better he would stop the tablets but it must be his decision, not hers or mine.

As it turned out, that last bit of advice was bad advice. I had to return to London on the Sunday night as I had appointments there on Monday, Tuesday and Wednesday, but I made arrangements to visit her on the following Thursday to continue with the healing.

Peter and his wife had also invited me to have dinner with them in the Hotel, on the Thursday after the healing session. I was worried about the Mother on the Tuesday afternoon, and telephoned to see how she was.

Her husband answered the telephone and he said "You cannot speak with her now, and don't bother to come on Thursday, you will not be welcome." The telephone was replaced with the words "I am very busy and I can't speak with you any more."

I rang John and asked him what it was all about. He could not help, but said he would find out and ring me back later that evening.

When John rang back I asked "For goodness sake what's it all about, what has happened between Sunday and now to make so much difference in your father's attitude?"

He told me "Ma had decided that as she felt so much better she would go shopping this afternoon" (just what I had told her NOT to do!). "While she was out, she tripped up the kerb, hitting her head and cutting her leg.

As she had no identification on her, an ambulance was called, and they took her to hospital.

The doctors there, none of whom knew her history, asked "Are you on any medication?" She told them the name of the tablets she was taking. Their immediate reaction was

"They could make you lose your balance quite easily", and they asked her if she had had any other treatment.

She told them "Yes, I had some healing on Sunday."

The doctors said, "You had what?"

Ma replied "I had some healing."

John continued "She was told that she must not have anything to do with these people. She was told to "stay away from these people. They are all cranks and quacks."

She was one of the old school who believe that doctors must know what is right for us. They must know because they tell us what to do. Our lives depend on them and she was too frightened to go against them in any way; and, after all, hadn't I told her to follow her doctor's advice!

John's brother had arranged for me to have dinner with him and his family on the Thursday after I had given his mother her healing. This was also cancelled. I was not allowed to visit her again. I do not know if she could have been cured with healing, but I do know that the quality of her life could have been made that much better. With healing, she could have 'lived' until she died, instead of dying until she died.

There is nothing miraculous about healing or any other form of mediumship.

It is simply the using of the natural faculties. What happens with healing is that the person giving the healing has retained contact with the source of power and life and is used as a channel to transfer some of this power to the one in need. Gathering in the power and giving it out to the one in need - this then starts the sick person's body working for itself. It is very much like winding up a clock which has run down.

People talk of a heat that seems to emanate from the healer. The healer's hands can be inches away and yet the person can still feel the power. When the body is sick the aura around that part of the body changes colour. If the person is very sick I see that aura as almost black around the sick part but if it is a minor problem then the aura is quite often only a light grey.

Each medium sees things differently and colours mean one thing to one person and something else to another, symbols are also quite often used to illustrate a point. The reason clinics like the one at Bristol work, is because they tell the patient to concentrate on 'seeing' the body whole and free from disease, directing the mind to control what is happening to the body.

The mind does control what goes on in the body. If we are told by doctors "There is nothing to be done, you will have to learn to live with it," that is what our mind accepts, and it will not direct the body to heal itself.

The body has every facility to heal itself given the chance, but it can only do what it is directed to do by the mind. If we don't have enough peace and quiet or natural sleep, the mind does not have the chance to put the body right. Drug-induced sleep does not allow the mind to work on, and heal, the body either.

The laws governing this are mysterious only while we remain ignorant of the facts. Knowledge removes the mystery, and allows us to see that all phenomena can be explained and understood when placed within the context of natural law.

When someone comes for healing, I can usually tell what is wrong and what the pain is like, because it is momentarily transferred to me, just long enough for me to understand what is wrong with the client.

During healing, it is as though I stand outside myself, watching what is going on, much as a spectator would.

I am constantly amazed at what happens, and how whoever is helping with the healing knows exactly what is needed and where to direct my hands. This following example may go some way to explain what I mean.

My cousin Will wanted to bring a friend, Alfred, who had been told by medical people that he had but a few months to live: one kidney had been removed and the other was now badly diseased. I did not know if he could be helped or not, and suggested that Will brought him to the house.

Will was to tell him they were coming for a cup of tea, and then we would see if anything happened. Will was instructed not to say anything about healing, just to tell the man that he was visiting his cousin and ask him if he would like to come along.

When they arrived, I made a pot of tea and waited for a sign so that I would know if he could be helped.

This takes a different form with each person. For a long time, nothing happened. I did not feel the urge to put on my Strauss music. The pain was not transferred to me, nor did I feel that I wanted to say anything or touch him - none of these usual phenomena occurred.

I began to feel very sad, as I thought nothing could be done for him, but then I found myself going to the kitchen and bringing back a wooden seated chair. I wondered why, but did it just the same.

Back in the drawing room I asked the man to sit on the wooden chair. It was explained to me later that it is always better if a wooden chair is used - wood does not retain other peoples vibrations as much as a padded seat.

He looked slightly puzzled but did as he was told. He said afterwards he thought it a bit strange but felt he must do as he was asked. I stood behind him and waited, my hands resting lightly on his shoulders.

He did not object or ask what was going on. It was as if he knew somewhere inside himself, that it was important for him to accept what was being done.

After a few minutes, my hands were guided to his middle back and this area was gently stroked for some time, my hands going down to the base of the spine and then to the middle back. It was as though the poison was being gently propelled to where it could be disgorged.

Then my hands were on his head, stroking and pushing gently, from there to his arm and leg, always fingers exploring, and 'looking' through closed eyes at what needed doing.

All this time he sat quietly, with his eyes closed, becoming more relaxed with each passing minute. This continued for a half an hour or more, until all had been accomplished.

I washed my hands in cold water - cold water is best as it does not open the pores of the hands and allow whatever has been removed from the client to penetrate through the healer's skin. NEVER use hot water.

I then drank a glass of cold water and took one in for Alfred.

When we had both recovered (yes, both recovered - it takes both patient and healer some time to come back to normal) I asked him,

"I can understand why my hands were directed to your back but why were you given healing on your head, and arm, and leg? Have you had some trouble with them?"

"Oh yes, my dear, I have, a great deal of trouble. My daughter was missing early last year and I went out with the police to try and find her and fell badly, hitting my head, and my leg and arm were crumpled up underneath my body. I have been in great pain since then. I didn't mention it to anyone because I didn't want to bother them when there has been so much concern over my kidneys. My daughter was found murdered later on. That's when my trouble began. I can trace it back to that time."

So again we find bitterness, anger, resentment all doing their dreadful work, poisoning the body, killing organs one by one just as if he had been drinking or taking poison orally.

My cousin helped me to take the tea tray back to the kitchen and I found myself telling him

"Alfred will telephone you tomorrow morning at 6.30 and say that he is in agony, and that he thinks he is going to die. He will ask you to go to him. You must go. He will not die. The pain will be caused by the body getting rid of all the poison from the kidney. He will be all right by 9 o'clock, and will not have any more problems. But please go and help him over those hours of pain."

When we got back to the drawing room, Alfred was pacing up and down saying,

"I feel warm. I feel warm for the first time in months. How can I ever thank you?"

He was told "Just say thank you when you say your prayers," and they went off home.

He did telephone my cousin the following morning and, of course, Will went to him. Alfred was sure he was going to die and very soon.

"I'm in agony, I know I can't last much longer, help me for God's sake please help me. I thought that healing had done the trick but now."

Will assured him that he would not die, the pain would ease soon and he would be fine.

"Just hang on and you will be out of pain in a couple of hours, then you will be free of it completely. Your kidney will be clear and you will be able to get on with your life."

He recovered fully, and went back to work at his building firm.

Years later I heard that he was still enjoying good health and I said a heartfelt thank you in my prayers.

FREEWILL.

When people ask to see the 'fortune teller' I tell them I am not a 'fortune teller.' To my mind, fortune-tellers are 'purveyors of hope' they will tell you just what you want to here.

NO one can say this or that will happen, not even God himself can tell us what WILL happen. He can tell us what COULD happen if we do this or that, but it is still up to us.

We can go any way we choose. We have free will.

All anyone can do is show us the opportunities that are always there in front of us. Or the pitfalls, (both of which we have made for ourselves by our thoughts, words and deeds,) then try and guide us in the right direction so that we can make the most of them in a constructive, rather than destructive, way.

Just as when we die, we see the whole of our past life flash before our eyes, so before we are born, we see the life we have planned, and chosen, for ourselves. A life where we will complete our Karma and evolve a little more spiritually.

We have chosen our parents, the most important people in our lives, the buildings we will see, everything that we will find on that path. The path that WE chose so carefully. But we are given free will to do as we please.

We know when we are on the 'right' path, the one we 'chose' before we were born, because everything falls into place like a jigsaw puzzle, and everyone speaks 'our language.'

This need not necessarily be a happy time for us; it may be that we need to be there in a painful life to learn something, or for someone to learn something from us. We meet someone for the first time, seemingly, and yet we know them so well. We enter a strange building and know just where that door will lead and what we will find, even though we have not been to that place before. You must know what I mean; you've all had those feelings at some time in your life I'm sure.

When we are not on that path, nothing goes right - '<u>NOTHING.</u>' No one speaks our language, and we seem to just drift through life.

There doesn't seem to be anything that we can pinpoint and say, "I'll change that, and all will be well." But still we have free will to do as we please.

You say "I would not have chosen this life of pain for myself," but sometimes we do choose a life of pain, to understand what it is like to be there.

If we have not shown sympathy or understanding to those in pain in a previous life, we will have to come back and be in pain at some time to balance natural law. At some time, we have to experience everything there is to enable us to become whole and rejoin 'The godhead.' This can take hundreds of lives or a few, depending on whether we follow the path we chose before we came to this earth, or just our own sweet way without thinking or listening to our higher selves.

Our left hand shows the life we chose, every second of our life is mapped out in that left hand. The right shows what we have done with that life. (If we are right handed that is.) One very rarely finds the two hands match, mine certainly don't! I think the statistics show it's about one in five million! Sometimes, it is a good thing to be told what lies ahead of us so that we can be open and aware enough to make the most of the opportunities as they arrive, and recognise them quickly enough to be able to do something with them.

But, even though we have been told, we need not KNOW there is such a gap between hearing and knowing. In that way, not knowing, we miss yet more chances. Opportunities are being created all the time by ourselves, and, by Spirit, and we neglect to take advantage of them. I include myself in this!!

They cannot make us see them; they cannot make us take the path we mapped out for ourselves. We all, as individuals, choose what we do every time!

WILLING A BOYFRIEND FOR WENDY

Wendy and I were walking along the Embankment one evening in March, and she said

"I would really like to have a boyfriend, someone who would be really, really special."

Wendy was an extremely attractive girl from a good family and working in London. Her family was still in Hebdon Bridge, and I think she was missing them.

She could cook like an angel, had all the social graces, and a good voice. Wendy also played tennis; in fact everything a man could want in a wife and mother but the right man had not turned up. There were plenty of young men interested in her, but no one who had stirred her heart.

I said, "Ok.let's will one for you, shall we? Let me see what will he be like?"

I paused then and said, "I know. He will have brown hair, curling slightly at the ends."

We walked a little further then, "And he'll wear glasses sometimes."

Another hundred yards and "He'll drive a sports car, and occasionally will have a large dog sitting in the back of it. Yes, he will also have a large carved chair with his initials on the back of it. The chair will be at the family 'seat.'"

Silence fell between us until we reached Blackfriars Bridge and sat down.

Wendy said "Anything else?"

I was about to tell her no, but instead went on to say "He will come from a good family and play the same sports that you enjoy. There is a tennis court in the grounds of his family home. His name will begin with 'P'."

I thought we were playing games, even though I had seen it all quite clearly.

Two months passed and Wendy was helping me to prepare for my birthday party the next day. She had made some of my favourite things for me; she is such a good cook. But she was looking quite sad as she said

"He hasn't arrived yet. I don't think he will."

I was prompted to tell her "Don't worry, he is already around. You don't have to wait much longer."

I thought it a rather strange thing to say when I had no proof and wondered where he could be.

I was living at number 12 and Wendy was in the kitchen there with me. She had a room in a flat at number 20.

She went along to her flat as she was expecting a cheque from her

156

mother. It had not arrived before she left that morning and she was hard up. She was back in five minutes, running up the stairs two at a time very excited.

"It's him, it's him!" she exclaimed. "I have just seen him, I know it's him. He has brown hair and glasses. I saw him through the hedge as he was going back into his house next door to mine. He had just put the letter from my mother in my letterbox. The letter had been delivered to No.22 by mistake. What can I do, what can I do? How can I get to know him? Oh, come on you must do something! Help me! Think of something."

"Calm, down, calm down. I know just what to do. We'll send him an invitation to my birthday party", I said.

"But we can't do that", Wendy said, "we don't know him, we don't even know his name. How can we send an invitation to someone if we don't know their name?"

"Of course we can. We will put on the envelope 'To the one who delivered Wendy's letter!' and you can take it and put it through his door", I said.

So that is what we did. Wendy ran and put the invitation in his letterbox, and as she was running out of the gate of No 22, he called her saying

"Did you put this envelope through my letterbox?"

"Yes", she replied.

"So your name is Wendy?"

"Yes."

"Well Wendy, I will be delighted to come to come the birthday party. Thankyou very much for asking me."

My birthday night came, and Wendy was one of the first to arrive. An hour later the party was in full swing when the doorbell rang again, and I went to answer it. There stood the one that I had 'seen' while Wendy and I were walking along the Embankment.

He said "You don't know me, but,"

I laughed. "Oh yes I do, I know you very well. Please come in, everyone is upstairs."

As he stepped inside, he said, "My name is Richard."

I stood quite still thinking 'Richard'? Oh dear, something has gone very wrong, his name is supposed to begin with 'P.'

"Richard Parker", he said, breaking into my thoughts.

(Not his real name, but his surname did begin with 'P'). I heaved a sigh of relief. So, he was the right one after all.

Richard and Wendy saw a great deal of one another after this. He took her to meet his parents in his sports car and when they were in the country his large dog accompanied them, sitting in the back seat!

The family seat in Hertfordshire had a tennis court in the grounds - all was as it had been 'seen' when we walked along the Embankment in March. Richard shared the house next door to Wendy's flat in Notting Hill Gate with J.B. - a stockbroker - and when Richard eventually went away to Australia, as he had to do so that the story could have a happy ending, J.B. comforted Wendy and they fell in love.

Richard had received a letter from the girl to whom he had been engaged before he met Wendy, asking him to go to Australia and the two families, Richards and hers, mutually agreed that he should go. Their parents had known each other for a number of years and shared business interests.

J.B. and Wendy married a year or so later and have three children now.

Richard is also happily married to the girl in Australia and they all remain good friends.

This story of how J.B. and Wendy met was told at their wedding.

Oh yes, one thing I almost forgot: at Richard's family seat there is a large carved chair with his initials on the back. So everything was as they 'The Management' said it would be.

WHY HASN'T IT HAPPENED?

Sometimes people come back and say

"It was said that this, or that, would happen and it hasn't, why not?"

We sit quietly and I ask why these things have not happened and it is always because the client has not done what they were advised to do if they wanted to be able to take advantage of this or that opportunity. For example—

One girl came back very cross, sometime after a reading, and said,

"It was said in the reading you gave me, that my husband would come back and stay. He didn't."

"Oh dear, that's bad, tell me what happened and what was said."

"You said he would come back in a few weeks."

"And didn't he?"

"Yes, he did."

"I see, so what happened?"

"He stayed the night and then went away again."

"What were you told would happen? Were you not told what to do if you wanted it to work?"

"Oh yes, you said I must be still and listen."

"And did you listen, were you still?"

"'Yes."

"So what else were you told?"

"I was told not to question him about a particular subject."

"And.?"

"Well, I didn't see that it would make that much difference after he had stayed the night, and anyway I couldn't stop myself."

"There, my dear, you have answered your own question. If you do not listen and act as you are asked then natural law cannot operate, and the opportunities slip by once more."

"Shall I invite him to come again?"

"No, not yet. If we let things go out of time it is no good chasing after them, we just have to wait for the right time to come again. Otherwise it is like chasing after the sea when it is going out, and trying to pull it back in again - it cannot be done. We just have to wait for the tide to turn naturally."

WILL I NEVER LEARN?

During the summer of 1975, I visited Norfolk and spent the last part of my final evening there talking with the owners of a pub opposite Norwich Station.

They promised to let me know when it was 10.15 p.m. I did not have a watch, and the last fast train to London, the one I needed to catch, left Norwich at 10.30.

They forgot until 10.29 p.m. I ran as fast as I could across the busy road through the huge car park, and into the Railway Station, but was just in time to see the train pulling away from the platform and out of the station. I went back to the pub, which was closed by this time, but, as I had raced out of the door in my desperate bid for the train, the landlord had said,

"If you don't catch the train, come back. The milk train doesn't leave until five to two, and you can't sit on the station all that time, you never know what might happen. Plus, you don't have a coat and it's getting pretty chilly."

It was decidedly chilly. I was wearing a sleeveless dress, no woolly or coat, so I was very grateful for his offer. I sat and chattered with them for some time while they did the clearing up. A very handsome young man walked in, fair-haired, tall and very broad. Where had I seen him before? He looked very familiar. The landlord greeted him as a friend. The man said he was travelling to London, and would I like a lift?

I asked the landlord "Is it all right? Will it be all right to go with him?"

He said the man was a customer who had been in the pub earlier that evening saying he was going to London and he was sure that I would be safe. This man had been in the other bar and had heard me talking with the bar staff, about having to catch that last train. I wondered whether they had conspired together and the landlord had purposely forgotten to remind me of the time, so that I would miss my train and this man could offer me a lift. I tried to put these foolish thoughts out of my head, but as we went out to the car park in the station I knew in my heart I should not go with him. What I call my 'little man in the head' was saying "Don't go with him, please don't go with him." But I justified my going with him by telling myself that I could not wait for the five to two milk train. I would not be able to get across London at that late hour and I wanted to get back to the hostel. If I had been thinking straight I would have realised that even if he drove like a mad man, I still would not reach London in time to get the underground train to the Arsenal. As we were driving out of Norwich, he was driving very fast. I was very frightened, and thought I could protect myself somehow by telling him that I had been talking to the police that afternoon. I spoke to them about a poster they had at the station showing a photograph of a missing girl. I had told them I thought I'd seen this girl in our day centre in Kingsway and they were going to telephone me the next day to give me more information about her. This was not strictly true. I had spoken to the police, but I was going to telephone them, not they me. I felt it was necessary to tell him this white lie as I felt so uneasy. I wanted him to think that the police would be concerned if they could not contact me. I had promised the police that I would talk with the girl and try and persuade her to return home. He slowed down until we were out of the town and then picked up speed again. I asked him,

"Why are you going to London at this time of night?"

"I am going to the docks. I work in the docks." He said.

"Where in the docks? What time do you have to be there?"

"The London Docks, I have to be there at four o'clock."

"Why are you going so early? Wouldn't it be better if you drove in later?"

"I like to go early, I'll have a kip when I get there." Adding, "Or on the way."

Now why did I think that sounded menacing? That last bit "Or on the way."

I asked him his name and he told me his name was Joe. As I felt so nervous I tried to keep up a constant conversation but found it impossible, and lapsed into an uneasy silence. I was terrified when he pulled onto the hard shoulder of the main road about an hour later. "Why are you stopping?" I asked, "Why can't we go on?"

"I'm going to have a kip," he said in his broad Norfolk accent.

"It would have been better for me to wait in the station for the train than to sit here, I want to get home, it's very late and I am tired."

There was no answer. I wound my window down as far as it would go. There was a full moon and I was thinking 'if I have the window open maybe someone will hear me if I shout.' I toyed with the idea of getting out and trying to walk back to Norwich or hitching a lift to the nearest station. But then I might find myself in an even worse situation. Oh my God, what can I do? By this time, his blonde head was resting on my shoulder. I tried to push him off but he would not move. Soon his hand was on my knee squeezing gently. I put it back on his knee but to no avail - back it came again - I told him.

"It's not going to do you any good, I don't play around."

He tried to kiss me. I wouldn't let him. I fought like a dog to get him off me.

"What's the matter, don't you like kissing?"

"Yes, I do like kissing but not with someone I have only just met and certainly not in these circumstances."

He tried hard to make me change my mind, found he could not get his own way, then he became very violent. He was massive and powerfully strong, it was exhausting me trying to fight him. I thought I am going to die, here in this van, I am going to die. There were a lot of cars going by and he seemed to suddenly become aware of this, stopped fighting me, put the car into gear and drove off at what seemed like a hundred miles an hour - but at least he was not fighting me any more. I was thanking my lucky stars and feeling very grateful for being saved when he turned off the main road down a narrow lane. No lights, and no other traffic. Now, I was really terrified. While we had been on the main road there was at least a chance that someone would hear me if I shouted loudly enough, but here? He stopped the car, grabbed me and tried to tear at my clothes once more. I fought and fought and was losing the battle. I asked silently "Please someone help me, please send some help." I found myself talking and listening to myself at the same time.

I was listening to a very strange voice but this voice was coming from my mouth.

"I have daughters older than you, haven't you any pride? You couldn't even have looked at me, I am old enough to be your mother."

This stopped him in his tracks, it made him stop, sit back in his seat and stare at me, and he seemed horrified. Did I look the way I sounded? I had no way of knowing. Was this the answer to my prayers? I took the opportunity to remind him that the landlord of the pub had seen us leave and many people would be concerned if I did not show up at the hostel the next day, and be just as concerned if I was injured in any way. He sat silent and still for some time, then he said

"Well, you can get out - just get out - I am not going to London. I never had any intention of going to London - you must have known that."

"How could I have known you weren't going to London? The landlord said he knew you and you were trustworthy. What else should I have done? The least you can do is take me to the nearest train station, you can see I don't have a coat and 1 don't know where I am. You obviously live here and know your way around. Please take me to a station, or at least drive me to where I can get some shelter for the night."

I was terrified and prayed for my safety and for forgiveness for not listening to my 'helpers' in the first place. He drove me to Thetford station, which was all in darkness, except for pilot lights. To get onto the platform we had first to go up some steps onto the bridge and then down the other side. I asked him to come with me to see if there were any staff about, pushing my luck a bit, but I didn't fancy climbing those stairs and finding myself being attacked by someone else on a dark station in the middle of the night. He went ahead of me, up the steps and down again onto the platform. He said

"I'll go and see if there is anyone about; you stay where you are."

A few seconds later I heard his car engine start up, and he drove out of the station yard and up the road, away he went at a great speed. He had obviously been here before, and had known he could get out from the other end of the platform. So that was why he was anxious for me to stay where I was. Shivering and covered with scratches, and bruises yet to surface, I stood and watched him go- but, joy oh joy, I was alive. There was a telephone box outside the station and I rang 999. I told them what had happened and how cold, tired and battered I was.

Their reaction was "Hard luck girl, you asked for it, you should not accept lifts from strangers. What else do you expect if you accept offers like that?"

I knew they were right. I should not have accepted a lift but that did not help me now.

"That's all very well and it is easy to be wise after the event, but what can I do now? It is twelve thirty. Is there a train coming through here tonight?"

"No there is nothing until the morning. The milk train goes through a different way. You will have to stay in a hotel."

The policeman told me where to find the hotel and then put the phone down, cut me off. He didn't bother to inquire whether if I had enough money to stay in the hotel, OR, if I was in a fit enough condition to get there. Luckily I had enough money and found the hotel easily. As soon as I reached my room I made myself a very large, strong pot of tea, sat on the bed shivering and decided the only thing to do was to have a hot bath to warm me up and ease the aches and pains. After breakfast the following morning I made my way back to Norwich and went straight to the pub where I had spent last evening. The landlord looked surprised to see me. He said,

"I thought you were going to London. What brings you back here so soon?"

"Yes, that is exactly where I should be, in London, but that fellow Joe, you know, the one you said was all right? Well, he had no intention of going to London or anywhere else. All he wanted was to get his way, no matter what the other person wants or doesn't want. He thinks anyone who accepts a life is an easy catch for him to do what he likes with."

By this time, my eyes were turning a nice shade of purple and my face, hands and arms were swollen and cut. I asked him to make sure that Joe didn't give anyone else a lift from there. I should have gone to the police in Norwich but I was afraid of another rejection and wanted to get back to the hostel. I was already a day late and had not made any arrangements for a stand-in for the Sunday. I had bought a paper at the hotel that morning. On the front page of this paper was a story about someone finding a girl's dead body which the Police thought, had been thrown from a car not far from there. This body had been found by the side of the main road. I thought,

"There, but for the grace of God, go I."

Why didn't the police connect the two I wonder? My distraught telephone call telling them of my horrific experiences the night before and a girl's dead battered body by the side of the road in the same area? If they did make any connections they didn't contact me. The hotel had my address so it would have been quite simple for them to find me.

This of course was yet another incident, which should have taught me to listen to my intuition. I know that if I have the slightest doubt about anything then I should not do it. I know when I am being warned. So many times I ignore this warning and get myself into all kinds of trouble and I miss many opportunities. Whoever takes care of us must be very patient and forgiving. I am eternally grateful for that.

KEITH MOON AND FRIENDS SHOW THE DANGERS OF BAD HABITS

I had a card from a young man who had been for a reading the week before. On the card he had written
"Thank you for sharing your gift with someone who was a misguided missile, and for putting me back on the right track. Love David."

I have seen him quite often since, and he has brought a number of people to see me. He says he was guided to my rooms, and even though he kept resisting, he was pulled back time and time again, until he came in. He was also 'taken care of.' He was told of things he had been doing which, if continued, would totally destroy him. He had been mixing with the wrong sort of people, and had been introduced to practices that were alien to him, and destructive to his mind and body. I E using drugs.

After the reading, he was able to see this for himself, and as he wrote on the card, had put himself 'back on the right track!'

During Michael's reading a young man came through. He would not give his name, but kept repeating. "Hey diddle-diddle, the cat and the fiddle, the cow jumped over the moon, the moon, the moon."

He continued, "'When I was on earth, I played drums; and created havoc on stage, breaking instruments and generally being very destructive."

He demonstrated this by throwing things about and making me dance around the room, much to my client's consternation. This young man went on to say that Michael's manager was his manager when he was on earth, and that he had something very important to impress upon Michael. I was shown the office from where the manager ran his business, and was asked to describe it in detail to Michael; to prove that what was being said was right. The door to the room was in the centre of one wall. This seemed strange to me doors are usually somewhere near the corner of the wall, aren't they? I was puzzled for some minutes, not being able to understand what I was seeing. The mans desk was immediately opposite the door. A book lay on the desk and the pages were being slowly turned to reveal dates and venues filled for months ahead, but, as the pages were turned, these dates were crossed out and 'CANCELLED' written through them. The young man who was communicating with us begged Michael to warn his manager of the dangers of 'the habit' which he said was responsible for the cancellations and forgotten appointments I had seen in the diary. He went on to say

"'He is a good man, the best, but because of 'the habit' he forgets that time is slipping by. He means to finalise arrangements but."

Two or three other voices joined the young man's, and added their pleas to his, please, tell him to stop. They shared a few 'in jokes' with my client, about the pop world, and then one of them they said they had to go. Another young pop star had just died from drugs, and they were needed to help him find his way.

My client was shaken by this communication. He told me that he had recognised the young man's identity by his repetition of the word 'moon'. This had been the boy's surname when he was on earth, and this was corroborated by his references to the practical jokes he was so fond of playing when he was on stage. He had died as a result of drugs, painfully, destructively. It was a great loss to the 'Pop Music' world as he was such a talented musician.

After Michael left, I spent some time clearing up my little room, putting things back in their places. All the time marvelling at the ways they find to prove who they were when they were here on earth, never satisfied with just giving a name, always proving beyond doubt by actions or words which only they and the client know about.

YOU MAY FOOL YOURSELVES YOU CAN'T FOOL US!

She came to my rooms giving a false name, was greeted by Spirit who then asked,

"What are you doing here? Your husband was here on Tuesday, giving his right name, and everything was explained to him in great detail. Go away and stop bothering us unnecessarily!"

She left, quite happy in the knowledge that someone was obviously looking after her, and aware of her doubts! She had given me a false name when she made the appointment to see if I would know she was connected with the man who had come on Tuesday, a Mr. Clark.

Later in the year, Mr. and Mrs. Clark came for a reading together, giving their right name this time. After some laughter over her previous visit, Mrs. Clark was reminded that it would soon be her birthday, and was told

"You will receive the most beautiful ring you can imagine - the ring you have always dreamed of getting."

She naturally thought her husband would buy her an eternity ring or something similar. Her birthday morning came and there was no ring, from her husband or anyone else. Later in the day, she and her husband attended the Family Planning Clinic, to hear the results of a pregnancy test they were anxiously awaiting. To their delight, they were told,

"The test is positive. You are going to have a child."

They asked, unable to believe their ears, "Are you sure? How can you tell when the test is positive?"

"The urine is mixed with a chemical and put on a slide. If the result is negative, nothing happens to it. If it is positive, a ring forms. You can see it for yourselves. Here is your ring - congratulations!"

The 'ring' Mrs. Clark thus received for her birthday was not the sort she or I had imagined, but it was certainly the best present she and her husband could have received. They had both been married before, and were longing for a child of their own to complete their happiness. During the same reading, Mr. Clark had been told that he would be offered a building, a building he must take.

"It will be the pot of gold at the end of the rainbow."

The building was described in minute detail and a drawing was done for him so he could not mistake it. Months later he telephoned me to ask if I would see the clients of another medium, a friend of his, who had been called away. I told him I could not do so, as at that time I was looking for somewhere to see my own clients. He begged me to accept his offer of any rooms I needed in his building.

"This is the building you said I would find, and it is the pot of gold at the end of the rainbow! There are hundreds of rooms here, and I want you to take your pick of them."

Unfortunately, despite many efforts to find a solution, it proved impossible for me to accept his offer. The building was a long way from my home, and without transport it was not feasible for me to use it for consultations.

It was right for Mr. Clark though, in every way. Mrs. Clark had the baby around Christmas time, and their happiness was complete.

Another client, John Miller, who came to see me around this time, was told very firmly,

"You will find the answers to many of your questions when you are introduced to Michael. Michael will take you to a restaurant with pink tablecloths, and you will order fish."

John was surprised at this cryptic message, and said vehemently, "I don't think so! I don't like pink, and I can't stand fish!"

But he telephoned me a few weeks later and said,

"Some friends introduced me to a person named Mike. I didn't connect this with anything you had said until later. Mike suggested that we went to his favourite restaurant. During the meal, I found that he, Mike, was aware of all my problems and had the answers to many of them. When I glanced around the restaurant I saw that I was surrounded by pink tablecloths. Then I realised I was eating lobster, which I adore. I had never thought of it as fish. So you were right and I am sorry for doubting you. Mike has proved to be very helpful!"

EMILY.

In the middle seventies Alan, the graphic designer mentioned earlier, married Valerie, who at that time, was a teacher. Valerie is a super girl and they have a good marriage. They now have two children, Emily and John.

I have always felt a special affinity with Emily. I am sure she is what some people refer to as 'an old soul.' There is so much awareness in this child; her parents have allowed her to retain those intuitive feelings, which are submerged in so many who are encouraged to become too sophisticated, too soon. She is far more knowledgeable than some people twice her age, but, she has kept her innocence. Her paintings in particular seem to show her continued contact with the Divine Love.

Most children, at some time or other, have what some parents call 'hallucinations' and play with other children not seen by grown-ups, but as they grow older the visions are dimmed. They leave behind the 'seeing's.' Eventually, the 'seeing's,' are suppressed altogether, because of what is considered to be their 'negative social value.'

"That will not help to impress employers or succeed in making a good impression socially!"

When we are still in the state of 'Divine Love' or awareness, as Emily is, we can, and do, respond to even a minute change in vibrations. We can 'see' how others feel and think.

Those in the more usual 'normal' state are stifled by the artificial barriers, which deprive them of the magic and inspiration of this awareness. They get into the habit of perceiving only what they can conceive; they fit sensations into their own limited view of what they should be, and all things are seen, not as they are, but as they think they should be. They receive so many sensations that they are forced to pick and choose, and then end up with a very limited view. They are deprived of so much.

It is like trying to play a sonata on only half of a piano. The consequent frustration is a direct cause of so much of the depression and disappointment seen in people by the medical profession today. When patients leave most doctor's surgeries they appear to be just as 'weighed down' as they were when they went in.

After a visit to a healer or a good psychic, they seem to be, and they certainly feel, several layers lighter. This is something that can be seen, especially by 'a sensitive,' but it is more felt than seen. They seem to have been lifted into a higher state of consciousness, and the usual heaviness of the body is diminished. They become less 'dense' and all say they are much lighter, 'walking on air' is how most of them describe the feeling.

One day towards the end of 1984, I had an overwhelming urge to visit Alan and Valerie. I was on my way to Eastbourne at the time, but I broke my journey to telephone and ask if I could call in. Alan said "Of course", and he picked me up from Redhill Station and drove me to their house in Reigate.

I had no idea why I had felt compelled to visit them, and the obvious good health and lively spirits in which I found them all, reassured me that all was well. I decided that, naturally enough, I had simply been missing them, and that being in their part of the country had made me long to see them again. Later, when I was talking to Emily, I noticed that she had a large lump above her front tooth.

"Does it hurt?" I asked her.

"No."

"Not even when you eat?"

"No."

"Oh well, that's all right then."

But I was still concerned, and when Emily had been tucked up in bed, I said to Valerie I thought she ought to visit a dentist as soon as possible. Valerie said that she would take her if the lump did not go away soon. I said, "Please do. I feel very strongly that it should be looked at as soon as possible, just to be on the safe side." I stayed with them overnight, and continued my journey to Eastbourne the next day.

Two weeks later, Valerie telephoned me, and said she had taken me at my word and paid a visit to the dentist with Emily the day after my visit. After a thorough examination of Emily's teeth, he explained that her two front 'milk' teeth were causing damage to the developing adult teeth, which were therefore impacted.

"If they are left much longer they will cause the adult front teeth to grow crookedly and cause great distress later in Emily's life."

He removed the offending teeth so that the adult ones could grow unhindered.

So there was a very good reason for breaking my journey that day and we were all very pleased that I had listened to 'my little man' in my head urging me to visit them.

I DECIDE TO WING IT!

In 1988 many things happened to members of my family and to close friends and clients who had become dear to me, some of which I relate here. I decided that I no longer wanted to work for, or with, 'The Management.' I was going to do something for myself, something 'OF' me rather than always 'through' me. I had always felt that I could not ask for money for readings, as they had nothing to do with me. 'I' had done nothing, I had just sat there and let words flow from me, words which I did not hear, being in a trance-like state at the time, and words which told of things I knew absolutely nothing about. Always 'through me' never 'of'' me. I began to think that 'I' could do nothing, and that 'I' knew nothing. I had not trained to do what I was doing, and if 'they' were not agreeable there was nothing I could do. I wanted to be able to say, "Yes, 'I' can do that." and not have to be always waiting on 'The Management's' say so!

This rebelliousness was brought about by first, my elder daughter's best friend being murdered a few yards from her door. He was the most important male friend she had, and the loss was devastating for her.

Then, my client Anne, who had been having healing, died. She had seemed to improve so much at first. Coming out of intensive care only a few days after having very major surgery for cancer, being allowed home after another week and astonishing the doctors and surgeons by what they called,

"Her miraculous recovery and the rapid regaining of her strength."

She and her dear friend David were able to do so many of the things they had planned over the years, and were looking forward to spending the next few years together. Then after a few months she began to have very bad pains in her stomach; it was thought she had an ulcer. It turned out to be more cancer and she died within days of going back into hospital.

Why? It seemed such a waste after all the effort she had made to stay here on earthy and continue with her life. She and David had so much to do, so much left to say. It was all made clear in a reading David had with me a few months after her death. Anne had been granted those extra few months so that she and David could sort things out between them, and do some of the things they had planned so often to do, but had always put off doing.

Soon after this, my younger daughter's longed-for baby died, leaving her in a coma-like state for days, and all of us desperately unhappy.

None of the devastating things that have happened to me personally have made me bitter or resentful, but these seemingly unnecessary events had the most drastic effect on me and I became very angry with 'The

Management.'

I decided that that over the years I had become unbalanced, not mentally, but unbalanced because I had been working purely on the Spiritual level and had completely ignored the material, which I now saw is as important, after all we do live in a material world!

I decided, "From now on I will look after myself, no more will I put everyone else first. I'm going to do something that will allow me to have the things I want, instead of waiting until I need them."

I saw young people of twenty owning their own houses, driving around in smart cars and being able to go on holiday whenever they wanted to.

I had none of these things. I didn't own anything, so I thought it was time that I looked out for myself. Why shouldn't I make whatever I could? I planned to earn a great deal of money, and spend it on things like a washing machine, a vacuum cleaner. I had neither! Maybe I'll have a holiday, something I had not had for fifteen years, simply because I had no money to spare for such things.

I was told about 'The Institute of Hypnosis and Parapsychology,' where they were necessarily, very money-minded, but, run by people who gave an excellent training course in Hypnosis and Parapsychology. So I signed-up with them, hoping it would help to make me more money minded. I completed my training and obtained my licence to practice as a Hypnotherapist.

I also did an extensive training course with 'Allied Dunbar' and got my licence from 'The Office of Fair Trading,' to work as a Financial consultant, Broker, and Debt collector.

I said to myself, "From now on I will never want again. No more will I have to wonder where my next meal is coming from."

The Hypnotherapy training was very good and I have proved to be an excellent professional consultant. But I found great difficulty in asking clients for the fee.

'Silly girl' I can hear some of you saying. Others, those who work with Spirit, will say, "Yes, I know that problem, it is always easy to ask for money for others, but not for oneself." But you see I was not asking for myself; all of the money I took, went straight to the Institute, to pay for training, leaflets, stationery, and the delivering of said leaflets - so why did I still find it so difficult? It was the same with my work as a financial consultant with Allied Dunbar one of this country's major financial houses. I could not tell the client his or her policy was going to cost X amount of pounds per month simply because, for me, being asked to pay that sort of money would have been like asking for the moon.

I had still not got my head round that money block; neither did I know enough about the policies I was being asked to sell. I had taken in just enough knowledge to scrape through the exams! I'd had to learn a new language, one totally alien to me, of 'discounted mortgages,' 'prospecting,' 'pensions,' 1,000's of K's, etc, just to get my licence. I now have no further commitments to either the Institute, (which is now closed) or Allied Dunbar.

I am very pleased with myself for having completed my training and passing both sets of exams to obtain my licences to practice as a practitioner in Hypnosis and Parapsychology, and as a financial consultant. In passing those exams I have proved to myself that I can do it, I CAN both study hard enough, and take and pass exams. Neither of which had I done until then!

Now I know that I had to be 'unbalanced' by achieving these firsts, to see just how balanced I already was. I had thought, and had been told by many, that as I was working purely on the Spiritual plain I must be unbalanced. They said, "You must balance things up by also working on the material plain."

How wrong can one be? I see now that it is entirely my own fault that I have nothing. I go around saying things like,

"I don't think I should make money out of the gifts I've been given, no one charged me for them. I just need to take enough to pay the rent, rates, and expenses."

If I say that's all I want, then that is all I will get! I know now that I have all the gifts, the training, and the intelligence, to make a success of whatever I want to do. All it takes is the will to make the right charges for my time.

I still have difficulty asking for my fees, I put notices up everywhere saying exactly what my charges are, but people STILL insist on asking "How much do I owe you dear?" It drives me mad!

I must tell myself firmly that I am not charging for my gifts, I am charging for my time, my LIFE.

I decided that it was time to get back to work on this book. This book, my life's story. The book, which was 'right' when first written, a ribbon ran through it and could be tied at the end.

Giles O Brian, a Publisher's Editor with Michael Joseph's, said he loved it and wanted it for publication, but asked for more.

He said, "I am sure it will be a best seller, a world wide best seller, but there is not enough here for a hard back, do you have more of the same?

"Oh yes there are hundreds of pages more." I said

He continued, "You haven't made enough of yourself Selena.

Neither have you done enough; you must expand elaborate. Make it more sensational, more extraordinary. Selena I'm sure you know that there are five million people out there in the world who will all understand what you mean when you say,

"He couldn't put a top on my head because he was seeing me in a Psychic way, as I am when I'm working." But there are five <u>HUNDRED million</u> others who won't. Explain. Your readers are going to want to know what effect all this is having on you, what's happening in your life while all these things are going on? What has it meant to you being used as a medium? How has it changed your life? And if not, why not?"

I tried to change it and make the manuscript as I thought Giles wanted it, but it didn't work I hated it, and so did he! I just did not understand what he wanted.

I couldn't explain what being a medium has meant to me, I was born this way I've never been anything else, so how could I say what effect it has had on my life, if any?

But now, as you can see, I have decided to put it in order, in fact, almost as it was in the first place. But elaborating on some things, explaining a bit more, saying how I felt as well as I can, tidying things up editorially but essentially it is now as it was when first hand written with the help of Spirit and my clients.

A lot of the incidents in this book will probably sound quite ordinary to you and I hope they do. The whole purpose of writing it as I have, with no claims of sensational happenings, or miraculous cures is to prove beyond a doubt just how ordinary, and natural these things are.

May your God go with you and bless your life, as my God has blessed mine.

A POEM FOUND IN MY GRANDMOTHER'S BIBLE.

Only a smile, yes only a smile,
That a woman o'burdened with grief,
Expected from you, t'would have given relief,
For her heart ached sore the while.
But weary and cheerless she went away,
Because as it happened, on that very day,
You were 'out of touch' with your Lord.

Only a word, yes only a word,
That the Spirit's voice whispered "Speak"
But the worker passed onward, unblessed and weak,
Whom you were meant to have stirred
To courage, devotion, and love anew;
Because when the message was given to you,
You were 'out of touch' with your Lord.

Only a song, yes only a song,
That the Spirit said "Sing tonight;
Thy voice is thy master's, by purchased right."
But you thought "Mid this motley throng,
I do not care to sing of the City of Gold."
And the heart that your words might have reached grew cold;
You were 'out of touch' with your Lord.

Only a note, yes only a note,
To a friend in a distant land
The Spirit said "Write!" but then you had planned
Some different work and you thought
It mattered little. You did not know
'T'would have saved a soul from sin and woe.
You were 'out of touch' with your Lord.

Only a day, yes only a day,
But oh, can you guess my friend,
Where the influence reaches, and where it will end
Of the hours you have frittered away?
The Master's command is "Abide in me,"
And fruitless and vain will your service be,
If 'out of touch' with your Lord!   Author unknown.